The Causes of War:
The American Revolution, The Civil War, and World War I

SCOTT FORESMAN PROBLEMS IN AMERICAN HISTORY

General Editors: **Edwin Fenton,** *Carnegie-Mellon University*
David H. Fowler, *Carnegie-Mellon University*

Volumes in this series:

THE CAUSES OF WAR:
The American Revolution, The Civil War, and World War 1
Kenyon C. Cramer

THE NEGRO IN AMERICA
Larry Cuban

LABOR IN AMERICAN SOCIETY
Raymond S. Iman and Thomas W. Koch

THE SUPREME COURT IN AMERICAN LIFE
Leonard F. James

AMERICAN FOREIGN POLICY
Leonard F. James

THE SOCIAL SETTING OF INTOLERANCE:
The Know-Nothings, The Red Scare, and McCarthyism
Seymour J. Mandelbaum

REFORM IN AMERICA:
Jacksonian Democracy, Progressivism, and The New Deal
Faye Rattner

GREAT DEPRESSIONS:
1837–1844, 1893–1898, 1929–1939
John Sperling

POLITICAL LEADERSHIP IN AMERICA
Emmett Wright, Jr.

The Causes of War

The American Revolution, The Civil War, and World War I

Kenyon C. Cramer, *Instructor of American History*
Shaker Heights High School, Shaker Heights, Ohio

SCOTT, FORESMAN AND COMPANY

COVER DESIGN BY ED BEDNO

Editors' Introduction

Growing numbers of history teachers realize that using source materials in their courses provides an added dimension of experience for their students. Total reliance on a textbook can no longer be considered an adequate means of learning history. Yet if the full value of documents and critical articles is to be obtained, they must be presented as something more than writings which record important events or as mere illustrations of what the text says. They must also challenge the student's ability to relate individual events to larger topics and to continuing themes in history.

Each volume of the SCOTT FORESMAN PROBLEMS IN AMERICAN HISTORY organizes source materials around one facet of our nation's past. A volume contains fifteen Problems, each designed for one day's work. In some of the books the Problems are intended to be read individually, at the proper chronological intervals. In others, they are grouped into three units of five Problems each, such a unit being best used as an uninterrupted week's work. Whether the Problems are studied individually or in units, they should be assigned only after the student had read the relevant material in his textbook.

One of the most vital services a collection of source materials can perform is to encourage the student to develop his critical abilities to the utmost in constructing historical explanations. Interpretation is the heart of history; the student should be brought to realize how essential it is to be able to do more with facts than memorize them. The SCOTT FORESMAN PROBLEMS are specifically designed to engage the student in the fascinating task of interpreting American history. Through them he will gain the skills and the enjoyment which come from reaching insight and understanding as well as knowledge of history.

Each Problem begins with an introduction written by the author to place documents in their historical context and to link together the Problems in a volume. These introductions prepare the student to read intelligently by defining the scope of the Problem, suggesting its relationship to larger issues, and pointing out difficulties of interpretation so that he will not attempt the impossible in generalizing from limited evidence.

The study questions at the end of the introduction carry the student further in applying the historian's critical tools. He may be asked to try to judge the reliability of a document or the bias of a critic, to assess an historical interpretation in the light of his knowledge, or to reason from particulars to a general conclusion of his own. Properly used, the study questions help beginning students find out what is important in source materials; without them, students often do not know what they are supposed to do with the readings.

To obtain more from a Problem than simply answers to the author's questions, the student should first read the introduction and questions and then pause to review what he already knows about the subject. Then, keeping the central issues in mind, he should study the entire Problem, perhaps first skimming through it to see the relationship of the parts to the whole, and then reading it carefully and taking notes. He will then be ready to consider his answers to the study questions in preparation for class discussion.

The teacher can use the SCOTT FORESMAN PROBLEMS in several ways. A Problem can perhaps serve most effectively as the basis for discussion by an entire class, with the lesson organized around the study questions or other questions proposed by the teacher to develop new points of view. What seems most appropriate for discussion will always depend partly upon the textbook used in the course and partly upon the instructor's own style of teaching and command of the subject. Each teacher should structure the discussion around those issues which he thinks are most important, but he should take care to link a Problem to those which precede and which follow it. These connecting links give the student the maximum opportunity to comprehend the theme of the volume. By treating a limited number of issues within each Problem, a teacher should be able to restrict discussion to one class period.

These volumes can be used in other ways. Many readings can serve as the basis for reports to the class by individual students. An entire volume, or a selection of Problems from a volume, may be used in preparing a controlled research paper; the three-unit volumes are especially suited to this purpose. The Problems may also be assigned as supplementary reading in those areas where text treatment is not extensive.

In the present volume, *The Causes of War: The American Revolution, the Civil War, and World War I,* Kenyon C. Cramer presents the interpretations of historians of the three wars. It is not surprising that historians writing soon after the events they describe are strongly influenced by their own attitudes toward those events. Historians writing long after the events are also subject to strong influences, generated by the conditions of their own times. How objective, then, is it possible to be in writing history? In examining historians' treatments of American wars, the student must face that question. And while applying historians' theories to his own knowledge, he must continue to face it in developing his own interpretations. *The Causes of War* brings to the reader a fresh appreciation of both the difficulties and the satisfactions of interpreting complex events.

EDWIN FENTON
DAVID H. FOWLER

PUBLISHER'S NOTE: The readings in this volume show capitalization and spelling of words, as well as sentence punctuation, as they appear in the sources from which they were taken. Thus, although the Problem introductions and headnotes are according to Scott, Foresman and Company editorial style, many of the readings are not. Omissions from the original texts are shown by ellipses, and interpolations, supplied by the author or editors for clarity, appear in brackets.

Table of Contents

Author's Introduction

This book, *The Causes of War,* is a study of the ways historians have interpreted the causes of three American wars: the American Revolution, the Civil War, and World War I. These conflicts were crucial in American history. After the Revolution a new independent nation was created. The unity of the new nation was challenged by events that led to the Civil War. Following World War I, the nation emerged as a great economic power and world leader. Historians have been zealous in their search for the causes of these wars, and although they have differed in their interpretations, their diligent research and fresh insights have added greatly to an understanding of how the three wars began.

Explaining the causes of any complex phenomenon is difficult because it is produced by so many factors, including those of mere chance or accident. Explaining the causes of wars is especially baffling because emotions and irrational behavior are nearly always important contributing factors. Some historians, therefore, have denied the possibility of finding "causes," and they accuse those who attempt to do so with oversimplification. The writer of history must continue to ask "Why?" if he wishes to gain an understanding of his world. Rather than abandon the search when he encounters difficulties, he must redouble his efforts to analyze and understand historical problems.

In his quest for objective explanations, the historian must guard against his own bias. He lives in a particular time and place in history. In countless ways, both obvious and subtle, his own times exercise an influence on him. Within this general setting he has a narrower "personal" history, involving, among other elements, his parentage, his schooling, persons who have influenced him, and the section of the country in which he lives.

Living in a particular time and place explains why a Southerner and a Northerner may write differently about the Civil War, but historical accounts which reflect solely the background of the writer are little more than prejudice and opinion. Two qualities raise good historical writing above that level. One is the historian's dedication to an objective search for the most complete factual record. The other is his skill in interpretation, which demands that he demonstrate a keen sense of proportion, unusual insight, and exceptional maturity of judgment. Historians should be judged by these high standards even though they cannot always meet them.

This volume, *The Causes of War,* concentrates on the way historians interpret history. It deals also with the writing of history in the profoundly important context of the causes of wars. There is no more serious problem in the modern world than the maintenance of peace. Wars in the past have been tragic but those of the future are unthinkable. If man wishes to avoid self-destruction, a better understanding of the causes of wars may help in some small measure to prevent future catastrophe.

As the reader involves himself in the clash of historical interpretations, the study of history becomes a stimulating exercise of the mind. The inquiring student who wants to know why things happened as they did will be encouraged to search out answers for himself. In so doing, he will learn from the professional historians that there is no substitute for diligent search for the facts and responsible interpretation as a prelude to the excitement of historical discovery.

KENYON C. CRAMER

unit one

The American Revolution

There is something magical about the moment of birth, something attractive about the beginnings of things and the circumstances which surround them. So it is with the birth of a nation. A people may naturally think of their origins as having been auspicious, even noble and grand.

George Washington, Thomas Jefferson, and Samuel Adams, Lexington Green, the great Declaration, Valley Forge, and Yorktown are the venerated names and symbols of the beginning of the United States and of the American Revolution which gave it birth.

The historian's responsibility is to see beyond myths and legends. In interpreting the causes and meaning of the Revolutionary War, George Bancroft, the influential nineteenth-century American historian, popu-larized the tradition of a glorious Revolution fought to preserve and to maintain human freedom. His works stressed the political aspects of this dramatic and stirring struggle. Bancroft's romantic nationalist history fulfilled a need for his day, but as time passed the American mood changed. Industrial growth, political reform, and a new emphasis on realism altered American attitudes. Historians developed a more detached, even skeptical point of view, while their interests turned to social and economic problems and to the study of institutions and group behavior. They began to study the American Revolution in terms of these concepts.

Excerpts from the writings of five historians are offered in this first unit of *The Causes of War* and present varying views on the origins of the Revolution. The reading in Problem 1 takes the position that the war was fought for the "rightfulness of human freedom." Problem 2 presents the argument that the Revolution resulted from clashing economic interests. In Problem 3 the selection interprets the Revolution as an episode within the broader framework of the British colonial system. Problem 4 emphasizes the role of agitators and propagandists, and Problem 5 reviews major interpretations of the causes of the American Revolution.

The explanations of these historians have raised many questions about the Revolutionary War. One is concerned with the impact of the British mercantile system, in which the economic interests of the colonies were subordinate to the welfare of the mother country. Did mercantilism cause the war? Another question lies in the sudden quickening of agitation after 1763. Did British colonial policy really change? Would the Revolution have come at all without the agitators and organizers? Of major concern also is the relative importance of economic interests and moral principles. What was really at stake? Was it self-interest, or was it liberty? or perhaps both?

In twentieth-century writing about the Revolution, historians have returned to the early emphasis on moral principles and "taxation without representation" as causes of the war. Some of this writing shows a "back to Bancroft" tendency though in a much more sophisticated form. In the nineteenth century, a period of great political tension, Bancroft's history constantly reminded the American people of their traditions and nationalism. If Bancroft met a need for his day, it is fair to ask what other historians represented herein have performed for theirs.

This question raises the issue of the historian's role and function in a rapidly changing modern world. His history must have relevance, otherwise the historian becomes, like Tolstoy's description of the academic historian, a deaf man replying to questions nobody asks. The historian cannot help reflecting his time and place in history, but at the same time he has a commitment to be objective. In examining the interpretations in this first unit, the challenge for the student will be to analyze the historian's function, to learn the extent of historical objectivity, and to find in the birth of the nation some meaning for himself.

PROBLEM 1

The Revolution
as a Struggle for Freedom

Much of the historical writing of the twentieth century on the American Revolution has been in one way or another a revision of the work of the famous nineteenth-century American historian, George Bancroft. The first volume of his *History of the United States of America* appeared in 1834. Subsequent volumes were published regularly until 1874, when the tenth and final one was issued. Bancroft's labors on this monumental work resulted in an outpouring of 1,700,000 words.

The life of George Bancroft embraced almost the entire nineteenth century—from 1800 to 1891. He was an ardent Jacksonian, and his writing was carried on while engaged in political activities and in serving at important posts. He was Secretary of the Navy and Acting Secretary of War in President Polk's cabinet. He held ambassadorships to Great Britain, to Prussia, and to Germany at various times during the administrations of Presidents Polk, Lincoln, Johnson, and Grant. He wrote President Andrew Johnson's first annual message to Congress. Because Bancroft was the first renowned historian of the United States, it is helpful to begin with his work in studying causes of the American Revolution. His exciting, romantic narrative of the American struggle for freedom and progress and his praise of the common man were popular with the reading public, and his books became best sellers in his time. His writing reflects the idealistic, nationalistic, golden age which produced Ralph Waldo Emerson, Henry David Thoreau, and Nathaniel Hawthorne.

Although Bancroft's thesis may appear naïve, idealistic, and sentimental to twentieth-century readers, his writings cannot be dismissed completely. A Harvard graduate trained in Germany where he received his Ph.D. degree, Bancroft combined the thoroughness of the professional historian with the enthusiasm and idealism of the literary romantic. He brought to American history writing not only a distinctive approach and flavor, but also a foundation upon which future historians could build their own schools of interpretation. As you read, consider these questions:

1 Should this selection from Bancroft be more properly classified as American literature rather than as American history? Could it be both?

2 What factual distortions do you find in the reading? Do they detract from the effect of the reading?

3 Does Bancroft offer any support for the British side? Was there another side to the story?

4 Bancroft claims that American patriots at Lexington and Concord "fulfilled their duty not from an accidental impulse of the moment." Do you agree?

5 The epitaph on the monument to Bancroft in Worcester, Massachusetts, reads in part: "Historian of America, he made it the high purpose . . . to show her part in the advancement of man, and . . . to ennoble the story of her birth." Do you think this is a legitimate aim for an American historian?

"A GLORIOUS MORNING"

This term, according to Bancroft, was used by Samuel Adams in referring to the morning of April 19, 1775, when Americans met the British at Lexington and Concord. The excerpt that follows was taken from the author's last revision of his ten-volume history. □ George Bancroft, *History of the United States of America, from the Discovery of the Continent*, Volume 4, pp. 152–160, 166. New York: D. Appleton and Company, 1887.

[General Thomas] Gage, who had under his command about three thousand effective men, was informed by his spies of military stores, pitiful in their amount, collected by provincial committees at Worcester and Concord; and he resolved on striking a blow, as the king [George III] desired.

On the afternoon of the day on which the provincial congress of Massachusetts adjourned he took the light infantry and grenadiers off duty, and secretly prepared an expedition to destroy the colony's stores at Concord. The attempt had for several weeks been expected; and signals were concerted to announce the first movement of troops for the country. Samuel Adams and [John] Hancock, who had not yet left Lexington for Philadelphia, received a timely message from [Joseph] Warren, and, in consequence, the committee of safety removed a part of the public stores and secreted the cannon.

On Tuesday, the eighteenth of April, ten or more British sergeants in disguise dispersed themselves through Cambridge and farther west to intercept all communication. In the following night the grenadiers and light infantry, not less than eight hundred in number, the flower of the army at Boston, commanded by Lieutenant-Colonel [Francis] Smith, crossed in the boats of the transport ships from the foot of the common to East Cambridge. There they received a day's provisions; and near midnight, after wading through wet marshes that are now covered by a stately city, they took the road through West Cambridge to Concord.

Gage directed that no one else should leave the town; but Warren had, at ten o'clock, despatched William Dawes through Roxbury, and Paul Revere by way of Charlestown, to Lexington.

Revere stopped only to engage a friend to raise the concerted signals, and two friends rowed him across Charles river five minutes before the sentinels received the order to prevent it. All was still, as suited the hour. The Somerset man-of-war [guarding the channel between Boston and Charlestown] was winding with the young flood [turning and twisting with the current]; the waning moon just peered above a clear horizon; while, from a couple of lanterns in the tower of the North church, the beacon streamed to the neighboring towns as fast as light could travel.

A little beyond Charlestown neck, Revere was intercepted by two British officers on horseback; but, being well mounted, he turned suddenly, and escaped by the road to Medford. Of that town, he waked the captain of the minute-men, and continued to rouse almost every house on the way to Lexington. The troops had not advanced far when the firing of guns and ringing of bells announced that their expedition had been heralded; and Smith sent back for a re-enforcement.

In the earliest moments of the nineteenth of April the message from Warren reached Adams and Hancock, who at once divined the object of the expedition. Revere, therefore, and Dawes, joined by Samuel Prescott, "a high Son of Liberty" from Concord, rode forward, calling up the inhabitants as they passed along, till in Lincoln they fell upon a party of British officers. Revere and Dawes were seized and taken back to Lexington, where they were released; but Prescott leaped over a low stone wall, and galloped on for Concord.

There, at about two hours after midnight, a peal from the bell of the meeting-house brought together the inhabitants of the place, young and old, with their firelocks, ready to make good the resolute words of their town debates. Among the most alert was William Emerson, the minister, with gun in hand, his powder-horn and pouch of balls slung over his shoulder. By his sermons and his prayers his flock learned to hold the defence of their liberties a part of their covenant with God; his presence with arms strengthened their sense of duty.

From daybreak to sunrise, the summons ran from house to house through Acton. Express messengers and the call of minute-men spread widely the alarm. How children trembled as they were scared out of sleep by the cries! how women, with heaving breasts, bravely seconded their husbands! how the countrymen, forced suddenly to arm, without guides or counsellors, took instant counsel of their courage! The mighty chorus of voices rose from the scattered farm-houses, and, as it were, from the ashes of the dead. Come forth, champions of liberty; now free your country; protect your sons and daughters, your wives and homesteads; rescue the houses of the God of your fathers, the franchises handed down from your ancestors. Now all is at stake; the battle is for all.

Lexington, in 1775, may have had seven hundred inhabitants; their minister was the learned and fervent Jonas Clark, the bold inditer of patriotic state papers, that may yet be read on their town records. In December 1772, they had instructed their representative to demand "a radical and lasting redress of their grievances, for not through their neglect should the people be enslaved." A year later, they spurned the use of tea. In 1774, at various town-meetings, they voted "to increase their stock of ammunition," "to encourage military discipline, and to put themselves in a posture of defence against their enemies." In December they distributed to "the train band [trained band of citizens] and alarm list" arms and ammunition, and resolved to "supply the training soldiers with bayonets."

At two in the morning, under the eye of the minister, and of Hancock and Adams, Lexington common was alive with the minute-men; and not with them only, but with the old men, who were exempts, except in case of immediate danger to the town. The roll was called, and, of militia and alarm men, about one hundred and thirty answered to their names. The captain, John Parker, ordered every one to load with powder and ball, but to take care not to be the first to fire. Messengers, sent to look for the British regulars, reported that there were no signs of their approach. A watch was therefore set, and the company dismissed with orders to come together at beat of drum. Some went to their own homes; some to the tavern, near the south-east corner of the common. Samuel Adams and Hancock, whose seizure was believed to be intended, were persuaded to retire toward Woburn.

The last stars were vanishing from night, when the foremost party, led by Pitcairn, a major of marines, was discovered, advancing quickly and in silence. Alarm guns were fired, and the drums beat, not a call to village husbandmen only, but the reveille to humanity. Less than seventy, perhaps less than sixty, obeyed the summons, and, in sight of half as many boys and unarmed men, were paraded in two ranks, a few rods north of the meeting-house.

How often in that building had they, with renewed professions of their faith, looked up to God as the stay of their fathers and the protector of their privileges! How often on that green, hard by the burial-place of their forefathers, had they pledged themselves to each other to combat manfully for their birthright inheritance of liberty! There they now stood side by side, under the provincial banner, with arms in their hands, silent and fearless, willing to shed their blood for their rights, scrupulous not to begin civil war. The ground on which they trod was the altar of freedom, and they were to furnish the victims.

The British van [or forefront division of the advancing troops], hearing the drum and the alarm guns, halted to load; the remaining companies came up; and, at half an hour before sunrise, the advance party hurried forward at double quick time, almost upon a run, closely followed by the grenadiers. Pitcairn rode in front, and, when within five or six rods of the minute-men, cried out: "Disperse, ye villains! ye rebels, disperse! lay down your arms! why don't you lay down your arms and disperse?" The main part of the countrymen stood motionless in the ranks, witnesses against aggression; too few to resist, too brave to fly. At this, Pitcairn discharged a pistol, and with a loud voice cried, "Fire!" The order was followed first by a few guns, which did no execution, and then by a close and deadly discharge of musketry.

In the disparity of numbers, Parker ordered his men to disperse. Then, and not till then, did a few of them, on their own impulse, return the British fire. These random shots of fugitives or dying men did no harm, except that Pitcairn's horse was perhaps grazed, and a private of the tenth light infantry was touched slightly in the leg.

Jonas Parker, the strongest and best wrestler in Lexington, had promised never to run from British troops; and he kept his vow. A wound brought him on his knees. Having discharged his gun, he was preparing to load it again, when he was stabbed by a bayonet, and lay on the post which he took at the morning's drum-beat. So fell Isaac Muzzey, and so died the aged Robert Munroe, who in 1758 had been an ensign at Louisburg. Jonathan Harrington, junior, was struck in front of his own house on the north of the common. His wife was at the window as he fell. With blood gushing from his breast, he rose in her sight, tottered, fell again, then crawled on hands and knees toward his dwelling; she ran to meet him, but only reached him as he expired on their threshold. Caleb Harrington, who had gone into the meeting-house for powder, was shot as he came out. Samuel Hadley and John Brown were pursued, and killed after they had left the green. Asahel Porter, of Woburn, who had been taken prisoner by the British on the march, endeavoring to escape, was shot within a few rods of the common. Seven men of Lexington were killed, nine wounded; a quarter part of all who stood in arms on the green.

Day came in all the beauty of an early spring. The trees were budding; the grass growing rankly a full month before its time; the blue bird and the robin gladdening the genial season, and calling forth the beams of the sun which on that morning shone with the warmth of summer; but distress and horror gathered over the inhabitants of the peaceful town. There on the green lay in death the gray-haired and the young; the grassy field was red "with the innocent blood of their brethren slain," crying unto God for vengeance from the ground.

These are the village heroes, who were more than of noble blood, proving by their spirit that they were of a race divine. They gave their lives in testimony to the rights of mankind, bequeathing to their country an assurance of success in the mighty struggle which they began. The expanding millions of their countrymen renew and multiply their praise from generation to generation. They fulfilled their duty not from an accidental impulse of the moment; their action was the ripened fruit of Providence and of time. The light that led them on was combined of rays from the whole history of the race; from the traditions of the Hebrews in the gray of the world's morning; from the heroes and sages of republican Greece and Rome; from the example of Him who died on the cross for the life of humanity; from the religious creed which proclaimed the divine presence in man, and on this truth, as in a life-boat, floated the liberties of nations over the dark flood of the middle ages; from the customs of the Germans transmitted out of their forests to the councils of Saxon England; from the burning faith and courage of Martin Luther; from trust in the inevitable universality of God's sovereignty as taught by Paul of Tarsus and Augustine, through Calvin and the divines of New England; from the avenging fierceness of the Puritans, who dashed the mitre on the ruins of the throne; from the bold dissent and creative self-assertion of the earliest emigrants to Massachusetts; from the statesmen who made, and the philosophers who expounded, the revolution of England; from the liberal spirit and analyzing inquisitiveness of the eighteenth century; from the cloud of witnesses of all the ages to the reality and the rightfulness of human freedom. All the centuries bowed themselves from the recesses of the past to cheer in their sacrifice the lowly men who proved themselves worthy of their forerunners, and whose children rise up and call them blessed.

Heedless of his own danger, Samuel Adams, with the voice of a prophet, exclaimed: "Oh, what a glorious morning is this!" for he saw his country's independence hastening on, and, like Columbus in the tempest, knew that the storm bore him more swiftly toward the undiscovered world.

The British troops drew up on the village green, fired a volley, huzzaed thrice by way of triumph, and, after a halt of less than thirty minutes, marched on for Concord. There, in the morning hours, children and women fled for shelter to the hills and the woods, and men were hiding what was left of cannon and military stores.

The minute-men and militia formed on the usual parade [or promenade], over which the congregation of the town for near a century and a half had passed to public worship, the freemen to every town-meeting, and lately the patriot members of the provincial congress twice a day to their little senate house. Near that spot [John] Winthrop, the father of Massachusetts, had given counsel; and [John] Eliot, the apostle of the Indians, had spoken words of benignity and wisdom. The people of Concord, of whom about two hundred appeared in arms on that day, derived their energy from their sense of the divine power. This looking to God as their sovereign brought the fathers to their pleasant valley; this controlled the loyalty of the sons; and this has made the name of Concord venerable throughout the world.

The alarm company of the place rallied near the liberty-pole on the hill, to the right of the Lexington road, in the front of the meeting-house. They went to the perilous duties of the day "with seriousness and acknowledgment of God," as though they were to engage in acts of worship. The minute company of Lincoln, and a few men from Acton, pressed in at an early hour; but the British, as they approached, were seen to be four times as numerous as the Americans. The latter therefore retreated, first to an eminence eighty rods farther north, then across Concord river, by the North Bridge, till just beyond it, by a back road, they gained high ground, about a mile from the centre of the town. There they waited for aid.

About seven o'clock, under brilliant sunshine, the British marched with rapid step into Concord; the light infantry along the hills, and the grenadiers in the lower road. Left in undisputed possession of the hamlet, they made search for stores. To this end, one small party was sent to the South Bridge over Concord river; and, of six companies under Captain Laurie, three, comprising a hundred soldiers or more, were stationed as a guard at the North Bridge, while three others advanced two miles farther, to the residence of Barrett, the highest military officer of the neighborhood, where arms, it was thought, had been concealed. But they found there nothing to destroy except some carriages for cannon. His wife, at their demand, gave them refreshment, but refused pay, saying: "We are commanded to feed our enemy, if he hunger."

At daybreak the minute-men of Acton crowded at the drum-beat to the house of Isaac Davis, their captain, who "made haste to be ready." Just thirty years old, the father of four little ones, stately in his person, a man of few words, earnest even to solemnity, he parted from his wife, saying: "Take good care of the children;" and, while she gazed after him with resignation, he led off his company.

Between nine and ten the number of Americans on the rising ground above Concord bridge had increased to more than four hundred. Of these, there were twenty-five minute-men from Bedford, with Jonathan Wilson for their captain; others were from Westford, among them Thaxter, a preacher; others from Littleton, from Carlisle, and from Chelmsford. The Acton company came last, and formed on the right. The whole was a gathering not so much of officers and soldiers as of brothers and equals, of whom every one was a man well known in his village, observed in the meeting-house on Sundays, familiar at town-meetings, and respected as a freeholder or a freeholder's son.

Near the base of the hill Concord river flows languidly in a winding channel, and was approached by a causeway over the wet ground of its left bank. The by-road from the hill on which the Americans had rallied ran southerly till it met the causeway at right angles. The Americans saw before them, within gunshot, British troops holding possession of their bridge, and in the distance a still larger number occupying their town, which, from the rising smoke, seemed to have been set on fire.

In Concord itself, Pitcairn had fretted and fumed with oaths and curses at the tavern-keeper for shutting against him the doors of the inn, and exulted over the discovery of two twenty-four pounders [cannons] in the tavern yard as though they reimbursed the expedition. These were spiked [disabled]; sixty barrels of flour were broken in pieces, but so imperfectly that afterward half the flour was saved; five hundred pounds of ball were thrown into a mill-pond. The liberty-pole and several carriages for artillery were burned, and the court-house took fire, though the fire was put out. Private dwellings were rifled, but this slight waste of public stores was all the advantage for which Gage precipitated a civil war.

The Americans had as yet received only uncertain rumors of the morning's events at Lexington. At the sight of fire in the village, the impulse seized them "to march into the town for its defence." But were they not subjects of the British king? Had not the troops come out in obedience to acknowledged authorities? Was resistance practicable? Was it justifiable? By whom could it be authorized? No union had been formed, no independence proclaimed, no war declared. The husbandmen and mechanics who then stood on the hillock by Concord river were called on to act, and their action would be war or peace, submission or independence. Had they doubted, they must have despaired. Prudent statesmanship would have asked for time to ponder. Wise philosophy would have lost from hesitation the glory of opening a new era on mankind. The train-bands at Concord acted, and God was with them.

"I never heard from any person the least expression of a wish for a separation," Franklin, not long before, had said to [Lord] Chatham [formerly William Pitt]. In October 1774, Washington wrote: "No such thing as independence is desired by any thinking man in America." "Before the nineteenth of April 1775," relates Jefferson, "I never heard a whisper of a disposition to separate from Great Britain." Just thirty-seven days had passed since John Adams published in Boston: "That there are any who pant after independence, is the greatest slander on the province."

The American revolution grew out of the soul of the people, and was an inevitable result of a living affection for freedom, which set in motion harmonious effort as certainly as the beating of the heart sends warmth and color through the system. The rustic heroes of that hour obeyed the simplest, the highest, and the surest instincts, of which the seminal principle [that is, having possibilities of future development] existed in all their countrymen. From necessity they were impelled toward independence and self-direction; this day revealed the plastic will which was to attract the elements of a nation to a centre, and by an innate force to shape its constitution. . . .

"From the nineteenth of April 1775," said Clark, of Lexington, on its first anniversary, "will be dated the liberty of the American world."

PROBLEM 2

The Economic Interpretation

During the latter part of the nineteenth century, Americans were pre-occupied with economic development in which realism and skepticism in thought made Bancroft's idealism seem increasingly old-fashioned. One powerful influence which focused attention on the material world was the theory of evolution formulated by Charles Darwin, the British naturalist. His studies concerning the relationships of living things to their surroundings renewed interest, particularly among historians, in the effect of environment on man.

Another influence was Karl Marx's theory concerning economic causation in history. Few Americans became Marxists, but Marx's views led them to consider economic relationships which Marx stressed as having fundamental importance. Marx believed that all history was a sequence of struggles between economic classes, and that inevitably a "classless" society would emerge.

Around the turn of the century, an American historical school appeared, which, though non-Marxist, interpreted history in terms of conflicts between economic groups. They emphasized the role of social and economic interests in shaping history. The most influential of these historians was Charles

Beard. His book, *An Economic Interpretation of the Constitution* (1913), while not directly concerned with the American Revolution, stimulated a re-evaluation of the entire Revolutionary period. Beard did not accept Marx's idea of inevitable class struggle, but concluded that the economic interpretation of history "rests upon the concept that social progress in general is the result of contending interests in society."

Four years before Beard's book appeared, Carl Becker had written *Political Parties in the Province of New York, 1760–1776*. In his book, Becker made the point that the American Revolution was not only a struggle against England but also a fight within the colonies—between radicals and conservatives. In other words, two struggles were going on at the same time. "The first was the question of home rule, the second was the question . . . of who should rule at home."

Arthur M. Schlesinger supported the interpretation that both economic motives and internal conflict had been important in setting off the Revolution. In *Colonial Merchants and the American Revolution* (1918) and in "The American Revolution Reconsidered" (1919), he argued that while the merchants, concerned with their profits, were the first to oppose the British, they were more alarmed by the democratic attitudes toward local government and civil rights that were spreading among the lower classes. Schlesinger denied that the Revolution was fought over consistent principles. He maintained that the radicals shifted from one position to another in order to get what they wanted. For example, such outcries as "taxation without representation is tyranny," he claimed, were mere propaganda rather than real grievances.

In the reading that follows, another historian, Louis M. Hacker, a specialist in economics, offers his interpretation of causes that led to the break with the mother country.

As you read, consider these questions:

1   Hacker states that "the past has a clear and inevitable logic." Do you agree? Would the study of the pre-Revolutionary period and the experiences of early American patriots necessarily be helpful in solving the problems of the United States in 1935?

2   If mercantilism was the cause of the American Revolution, as Hacker contends, how would it account for participation in the struggle by a number of social and economic groups?

3   Hacker's interpretation presumes that economic motivation is paramount in man. Does the selection from his book in the following reading bring out this presumption?

4   Is it possible that both Bancroft and Hacker are correct in their approaches to the causes of the American Revolution?

"THE FIRST AMERICAN REVOLUTION"

In approaching the cause of the American Revolution, the modern historian, Louis M. Hacker, is as far from Bancroft as London is from Lexington Green. Hacker sees the struggle to free American capitalism from British mercantilism as "The First American Revolution." In the following excerpt, Hacker analyzes the effects of British mercantilism upon New England and upon the Southern colonies. □ Louis M. Hacker, "The First American Revolution." New York: *Columbia University Quarterly,* Volume 27, 1935, pp. 260, 261–263, 265, 267–268, 269, 270–271, 272–274, 275–277, 279, 281, 288–290. Copyright © 1935 by Columbia University Press.

Many historians, today, in trying to plumb the mystery of the American Revolution, seem to be quite as ingenuous in their approach as Parsons Weems, the redoubtable creator of the Washingtonian myth. To the good preacher the reason for American revolt was altogether simple: the colonies were being plundered to take care of the royal poor relations and to feed the insatiable appetites of the ministers surrounding the English throne. Such an explanation . . . undoubtedly serves an important patriotic function when all the issues of the struggle have not been yet resolved, but obviously it will not do long after passions have cooled. . . .

Also, to see the Revolution simply as a struggle for democratic rights in the political sphere . . . is to make confusion only worse confounded. Nor is it possible to regard the struggle as arising out of a change in English colonial policy . . . . We shall see . . . that the break took place not because of the inauguration by England of a new policy but because the sharpening of the contradictions that lay at the heart of mercantilism had to tear asunder the imperial-colonial relations.

Finally, scholars find refuge in an obscurantism [that is, obscuring or preventing enlightenment] that is difficult to penetrate; and there is nothing more surprising than to see Professor [Charles M.] Andrews, who has done so much to clarify the nature of the commercial relations existing between England and its colonies, adopting such a position. The following is . . . [Andrews'] argument. For one hundred and fifty years, from the very hour of settlement itself, mother country and colonies had been growing farther and farther apart psychologically and institutionally. England was "an old, well-settled, highly organized lane"; its social and economic life had hardened into iron-bound molds; its ruling class, seated on its great estates and in firm possession of all the citadels of privilege, was guided by "rigid and sinister ideas of power and government." The colonies, on the other hand, were youthful, growing, and filled with "a frontier people instinct with individualism and possessed of but a rudimentary sense of obligation and duty." Thus, it really was the old, old struggle between aristocracy and democracy, between settled areas, with an ancient culture and a caste tradition, and the frontier with a fluid institutional life and a passionate belief in egalitarianism. The magical concept of the frontier, it seems, will explain everything to American historians. What if class divisions were as sharply drawn in the colonies as in England, that the colonial merchants and their legal spokesmen were as contemptuous of "mobsters" as were their English counterparts, that colonial planters settled on their broad acres in Virginia, Maryland and South Carolina lived as much in the aristocratic tradition as noble lords with estates in Surrey and Kent? All this, apparently, is irrelevant. The frontier made Americans free and out of this individualism was engendered a spirit of liberty.

In the face of these conflicting and implausible theories of learned scholars, bewilderment on the part of the uninformed is only natural. Unless we are prepared to start out with the premise that the economic and social relations . . . of the day, that is to say, mercantilism, no longer could be maintained, then the whole history of the critical period that preceded the American Revolution is simply unintelligible. . . . But because the past has a clear and inevitable logic, our study of this period in America's development is of the greatest contemporary significance because we, today [1935], living as we do in an era of productive decline, class oppressions and approaching crisis,[1] have much to learn from the ways employed by American patriots of an earlier time in the resolution of their perplexities.

The economic program the rulers of England adopted following the successful termination of the Puritan Revolution of 1641–49 . . . we have come to call mercantilism. What mercantilism was, simply, was a policy to assure the continued advance of English merchant, or pre-industrial, capitalism . . . . In this sense, therefore, mercantilism had two faces: at home it utilized the agency of the state to strengthen the position of commercial enterprisers in trade, manufacturing and agriculture; and abroad, particularly in the colonial relations, it . . . attached the oversea possessions in a subordinate capacity to the economy of the mother country. We shall not understand the character of the American crisis of 1763–1775 unless we are prepared to hold ever in mind the fact that every imperial administrative program . . . was designed to further this end: to utilize the colonies as an economic appanage [or source of revenue] of the mother country. . . .

[1]Hacker is referring to the great depression of the 1930's and to international problems created by the rise of dictatorships.

As regards encouragement of trade, the devices employed by the English government are well known. The Navigation System, reinaugurated in 1650, had as its initial purpose the wresting of sea power away from the Dutch; but its subsequent extensions were openly designed to shut down English ports to foreign ships. The intention behind the policy was the building up of the English merchant marine and the creation of a national monopoly of the carrying trade . . . .

The whole purpose of the Acts of Trade and Navigation was this design to keep in balance the economic relations between mother country and colonies; and all the administrative devices utilized had the same function in the social and legal spheres. Outstanding among the methods employed to assure the flow of colonial raw materials into the English market was that known as the enumeration of articles, as a result of which certain commodities might be exported only to England. In the act of 1660, the first list of enumerated articles contained sugar, tobacco, ginger, cotton-wool and fustic and other dyewoods; in an act of 1706, rice, naval stores, hemp, masts and yards were added to the list; in 1722, copper ore and beaver and other furs were included; in 1733, molasses was listed; and in 1764, whale fins, hides, iron, lumber, raw silk and potash and pearl ashes were enumerated.

On a second front, control over the colonial economy was pressed through prohibitions against the establishment of local manufactures. This had two effects: it prevented English capital surpluses from being invested in the colonies in large-scale industry, diverting them largely into land speculation and commercial agriculture; and it similarly prevented colonial surpluses from finding outlets in industrial enterprise, diverting them into commercial, or trading, activities. The placing of insuperable obstacles in the way of the employment of capital in the expansive field of colonial manufactures was undoubtedly the outstanding reason for breakdown in the imperial-colonial relations and the bringing on of the revolutionary crisis that led to the War of Independence. By specific enactment, in 1699, Parliament sought to check the development of a colonial woolen industry by forbidding the entrance of colonial wool, woolen yarn and woolen manufactures into foreign or intercolonial commerce. In 1732, similar action was taken in the case of the growing colonial hat-making industry by preventing the exportation of hats out of the separate colonies and by restricting colonial hat makers to two apprentices. In 1750, colonials were denied the right to extend the manufacture of wrought iron . . . .

The economy of the Southern continental colonies was based on the commercial production of a number of raw materials, or staples, vital to the continuance of merchant capitalism in England. These were tobacco, rice, furs, naval stores and indigo. The most important of these, of course, was tobacco and, as we have seen, the English monopolized the tobacco trade by requiring that the whole Southern crop be shipped only to English ports. Throughout the eighteenth century, as the Southern tobacco crop grew larger and larger, the unit price in London tended to drop periodically below the cost of production; in addition, capital costs of plantation operation mounted due to the high cost of labor (the price of indentured servants and more particularly that of slaves went up while their productivity remained constant), the exhaustion of the soil in the older regions, and the necessity on the part of the planters to buy new lands . . . .

Thus, virtually from the beginning, the plantation system was conducted on a narrow margin of profit . . . . What sustained the Southern plantation economy? It was nothing else than the presence of easily preempted lands in the wilderness areas . . . which planters were able to buy up for speculative purposes. The ability of planters to make a profit (. . . in their role as speculative landlords) furnished the incentive for the flow of short-term capital from England into the Southern colonies . . . . And short-term borrowings were converted into long-term indebtedness by the placing of mortgages on plantations and slaves. When these profits from speculative land operations threatened to disappear the flow of English credit ceased: and Southern planters were confronted by wholesale bankruptcy. . . .

But the English (and the Scotch, in this case) had also learned to regard with more than a curious interest these wild lands of the west: they saw in them opportunities for profits from the fur trade and from the speculative exploitation of the region by their own capitalist enterprise. It was at this point that English and American merchant capitalism came into conflict and when, as a result of the promulgation of the Proclamation Line of 1763 and the Quebec Act of 1774, the western lands were virtually closed to colonial enterprising, Southern merchant capitalism began to totter on its throne. Without the subsidiary activity of land speculation, the planting economy could not continue solvent; there is no cause for wonder therefore that Southern planters were among the first to swell the ranks of the colonial revolutionary host. . . .

The Northern economy in its capitalist relations was based chiefly . . . on trade. The Northern colonies directly produced little of those staples that England required . . . .

The Northern colonies, therefore, produced little for direct export to England . . . . They were buying increasing quantities of English drygoods, hardware and house furnishings, and were thus heavy debtors . . . in the

direct trade. Also—and this is an economic factor of the utmost significance—
the Northern colonies never, to any appreciable extent, presented important
opportunities for English capital investment. . . . The result was the imperative necessity for the Northern colonies to develop returns in order to obtain
specie [gold or silver coin] and bills of exchange with which to balance
payments in England. . . .

The trade with the West Indian sugar islands . . . became the cornerstone of the Northern colonial capitalist economy. Northern merchants,
loading their small swift ships with all those necessaries the sugar planters
of the West Indies were economically unable to produce—work animals for
their mills; lumber for houses and outbuildings; staves, heads and hoops for
barrels; flour and salted provisions for their tables; and low-grade fish for
their slaves—made regular runs from Salem, Boston, Bristol, Newport, New
York and Philadelphia originally to the British islands of Barbados, the
Leeward Islands and Jamaica, and then increasingly to the French, Spanish,
Dutch and Danish islands and settlements dotting the Caribbean. Here they
acquired in return specie for the payment of their English balances, indigo,
cotton, ginger, allspice and dyewoods for transshipment to England and,
above all, sugar and molasses for conversion into rum in the distilleries
of Massachusetts and Rhode Island. It was this wondrous alcoholic beverage
that served as the basis of the intercourse between the Northern colonies
and the African coast: and in return the Northern traders picked up ivory,
gums and beeswax and, most important of all, Negro slaves which were
again carried to the sugar islands on the famous Middle Passage to furnish
the labor supply without which the sugar plantation economy could not
survive. . . .

Smuggling also contributed its share to swell the remittances the Northern
merchants so badly needed. Smuggling traffic could be carried on in a number
of directions. In the first place, there was the illegal direct intercourse between
the colonies and European countries in the expanding list of enumerated
articles; and in the second place, ships on the home-bound voyages from
Europe or from the West Indies brought large supplies of drygoods, silk,
cocoa and brandies into the American colonies without having declared them
at English ports and paid the duties. Most important of all, of course, was
the trade with the foreign West Indian sugar islands which was rendered
illegal, after 1733, as a result of the imposition of the Molasses Act . . . .
It is imperative that something be said of the productive system and the
social and economic relations prevailing in the sugar islands, for just as
the western lands constituted the Achilles heel of the Southern planting
economy so the trade with the sugar islands—and notably that with the

tax measures among a liberty-loving and individualistic colonial people which too long had been permitted to go its own way. So Mr. Beer, and after him virtually every American colonial scholar.

The events of 1763–1775 can have no meaning unless we understand that the character of English imperial policy was never changed: that Pitt and his successors at Whitehall were following exactly the same line that Cromwell had laid down more than a century before; that the purpose of the general program was to protect the English capitalist interests which now were being jeopardized as a result of the intensification of colonial capitalist competition; and that English statesmen yielded quickly when a fundamental principle was not at stake and only became more insistent when one was being threatened. If in the raising of a colonial revenue lay the heart of the difficulty, how are we to account for the quick repeal of the Stamp Tax and the Townshend Acts and the lowering of the molasses duty? And, on the other hand, how are we to account for the tightening of enforcement of the Acts of Trade and Navigation at a dozen and one different points, the passage of the Currency Act, the placing of iron on the enumerated list, English seizure of control of the wine trade, and the attempt to give the East India Company a monopoly over the colonial tea business? The struggle was not over high-sounding political and constitutional concepts: over the power of taxation and, in the final analysis, over natural rights: but over colonial manufacturing, wild lands and furs, sugar, wine, tea and currency, all of which meant, simply, the survival or collapse of English merchant capitalism within the imperial-colonial framework of the mercantilist system.

The Imperialist School

During the greater part of the nineteenth century American history was not written by professionally trained historians. As a matter of fact, the study of American history was hardly regarded as a special area of scholarship but rather as an offshoot of European history. Not until 1884 was the American Historical Association founded.

In the late nineteenth century German scholars and historians began to discard narrative history for the study of "institutions," such as mercantilism, capitalism, and imperialism. The work of Leopold von Ranke (1795–1886) marked a turning point in modern historiography. His famous seminars in Europe taught "scientific" research and a commitment to laborious factual investigation. Ranke and his followers believed it possible to reconstruct the past as it actually was through systematic and painstaking research.

German scholarship had a great influence on a group of American historians in their approach to the study of colonial and Revolutionary history. George Louis Beer, Charles M. Andrews, and Lawrence H. Gipson, notable among this group, wrote massive, multivolume works filled with minute detail. They attempted to be wholly impartial and objective in their writing and studied the British colonial system from London rather than from Boston or Jamestown. Working in an era of increasing Anglo-American friendship, their sympathy with English colonial problems contrasted greatly with the views of a nationalist historian like Bancroft.

Charles M. Andrews, though not uncritical of the English policy, wrote American colonial history as if it were part of the history of the empire. In *The Colonial Period of American History* (1934–1938), he charged Louis M. Hacker with choosing facts to fit his thesis and argued that no amount of manipulation could prove that the British government operated solely in the interests of British merchants. Andrews felt that freedom from outside control became the leading issue after 1770 and that this issue involved much more than trade and commerce. "It is too great a simplification of history," Andrews wrote, "to regard the events of the past as nothing but a struggle of classes, a clash of economic interests . . . . To emphasize the economic aspects to the exclusion of all else is to interpret human affairs in terms of material things only . . . ."

In his 1926 address to the American Historical Association, Andrews reflected the influence of the frontier interpretation made popular by Frederick Jackson Turner in the 1890's. Turner held that the frontier experience was a primary force in the shaping of American history. In its frontier setting, said Andrews, the American colonies became a dynamic, expansive, self-governing society whereas England remained conservative, static, and increasingly "empire-minded." Within the empire there was a gradual evolution of a free American frontier society inevitably tending to break away from English restrictions. Thus, Andrews maintained, the Revolution began when the first settler came to American shores.

Andrews' pupil, Lawrence Henry Gipson, continued the imperial perspective of colonial history . . . .

The empire historians were characterized by their careful research methods, a sympathetic attitude toward England, and a belief that the Revolution could not be understood unless it was placed in the setting of British colonialism. As scientific historians, they passed on to the profession ideals of careful scholarship, arduous industry, and a disciplined effort to allow no intrusion of merely personal reactions. No historian after them could safely write about the American Revolution without taking into account the British side of the argument. In the reading that follows, Gipson discusses the importance of the French and Indian War and its relationship to the American Revolution. As you read, consider these questions:

1 How do the theses of Hacker and Gipson compare in their interpretation of changes in British policy after 1763?

2 Gipson declares that the settlement of the French and Indian

War "is perhaps the most momentous event in the life of the English-speaking people in the New World." Do you agree?

3 Gipson states that colonists reacted more violently against the older trade acts than against the stamp tax. Does he thus support Hacker's position that mercantilism lay at the root of the struggle for independence?

4 If Gipson's insistence on the title "Great War for the Empire" is justified, how can he, at the same time, claim that the acquisition of Canada was for the protection of American colonists?

5 Had Canada remained French after the "Great War for the Empire," do you think the American Revolution would have come as it did? that it would have come at all?

AFTERMATH OF THE GREAT WAR FOR THE EMPIRE

The eighteenth century, particularly those years immediately preceding the American Revolution, has been the center of interest for Lawrence Gipson. One of his chief objectives in writing in this field has been to demonstrate that all history should be presented in context. Hence, his placement of the War for Independence within the wider scope of British imperial history. □ Lawrence H. Gipson, "The American Revolution as an Aftermath of the Great War for the Empire, 1754–1763," New York: *Political Science Quarterly,* Volume 65, pp. 86–87, 89–90, 93–95, 96–101, 102–104. Copyright © 1950 Academy of Political Science.

Great wars in modern times have too frequently been the breeders of revolution. The exhausting armed struggles in which France became engaged in the latter half of the eighteenth century led as directly to the French Revolution as did the First World War to the Russian Revolution; it may be said as truly that the American Revolution was an aftermath of the Anglo-French conflict in the New World carried on between 1754 and 1763. This is by no means to deny that other factors were involved in the launching of these revolutionary movements. Before proceeding with an analysis of the theme of this paper, however, it would be well to consider the wording of the title given to it.

. . . [The] chief task of the historian is to illuminate the past. He is faced, therefore, with the responsibility of using only such words as will achieve this broad objective . . . and to reject those that obscure or defeat it. For this reason "the French and Indian War", as a term . . . , has been avoided in this essay . . . . In contrast to this traditional interpretation of our history one may affirm that the Anglo-French conflict settled nothing less than the incomparably vital question as to what civilization . . . would arise in the great Mississippi basin and the valleys of the rivers draining it . . . . The determination of this crucial issue is perhaps the most momentous event in the life of the English-speaking people in the New World and quite overshadows in importance both the Revolutionary War and the later Civil War, events which, it is quite clear, were each contingent upon the outcome of the earlier crisis.

A struggle of such proportions, involving tremendous stakes, deserves a name accurately descriptive of its place in the history of the English-speaking people, and the title "the French and Indian War", as suggested, in no way fulfills this need. For the war was not, as the name would seem to imply, a conflict largely between English and French New World colonials and their Indian allies, nor was it localized in North America to the extent that the name would appear to indicate. . . .

. . . John Fiske, the philosopher-historian . . . happily fastened upon the name "the Great War". In the series on the *British Empire before the American Revolution* the writer has built upon Fiske's title and has called it "the Great War for the Empire" in order to emphasize not only the fact that the war was a very great conflict . . . , but also, as a war entered into specifically for the defense of the British Empire, that it was by far the most important ever waged by Great Britain to this end.

It may be pointed out that later charges, especially by American writers, that the war was begun by Great Britain with less worthy motives in mind, are not supported by the great mass of state papers and the private correspondence of British statesmen responsible for making the weighty decisions at the time . . . . In other words, the idea that the war was started as the result of European balance-of-power politics or by British mercantilists for the purpose of destroying a commercial rival . . . must be dismissed by students brought face to face with impressive evidence to the contrary.

The development of the war into one for the military mastery of the North American continent came with the growing conviction on the part of the British ministers that nothing short of this drastic step would realize the primary aims of the government in arriving at the determination, as the result of appeals from the colonies for assistance, to challenge the right of French troops to be planted well within the borders of the Nova Scotia peninsula and at the forks of the Ohio. . . .

. . . [The] most fateful aftermath of the Great War for the Empire . . . grew out of the problem of the control and support not only of the vast trans-Appalachian interior . . . but of the new acquisitions in North America secured from France and Spain. Under the terms of the royal Proclamation of 1763, French Canada to the east of the Great Lakes was organized as the Province of Quebec; most of old Spanish Florida became the Province of East Florida; and those areas, previously held by Spain as well as by France to the west of the Apalachicola and to the east of New Orleans and its immediate environs, became the Province of West Florida. The Proclamation indicated that proper inducements would be offered British and other Protestants to establish themselves in these new provinces. With respect to the trans-Appalachian region, however, it created there a temporary but vast Indian reserve by laying down as a barrier the crest of the mountains beyond which there should be no white settlement except by specific permission of the Crown.

The Proclamation has been represented not only as a blunder, . . . but also as a cynical attempt by the British ministry to embody mercantilistic principles in an American land policy that in itself ran counter to the charter limits of many of the colonies and the interests in general of the colonials. Nevertheless, this view of the Proclamation fails to take into account the fact that it was the offspring of the war and that the trans-Appalachian aspects of it were an almost inevitable result of promises made during the progress of hostilities. For both in the Treaty of Easton in 1758 with the Ohio Valley Indians, a treaty ratified by the Crown, and in the asseverations of such military leaders as Colonel [Henry] Bouquet, these Indians were assured that they would be secure in their trans-Appalachian lands as a reward for deserting their allies, the French. As a sign of good faith, the lands lying within the bounds of Pennsylvania to the west of the mountains, purchased by the Proprietors from the Six Nations in 1754, were solemnly released. Thus committed in honor in the course of the war, what could the Cabinet Council at its termination do other than it finally did in the Proclamation of 1763? But this step not only was in opposition to the interests of . . . land speculators . . . , but also led to open defiance of this imperial regulation by frontiersmen who, moving beyond the mountains by the thousands, proceeded to settle within the Indian reserve . . . .

The Proclamation line of 1763 might have become an issue, indeed a most formidable one, between the government of Great Britain and the colonials, had not the former acquiesced in the inevitable and confirmed certain Indian treaties that provided for the transfer of much of the land which had been the particular object of quest on the part of speculators and of those moving westward from the settled areas to establish new homes. . . .

The British ministry, thus confronted with the problem of guaranteeing the necessary security for the extended empire in North America, which it was estimated would involve the annual expenditure of from three to four hundred thousand pounds for the maintenance of ten thousand troops . . . was impelled to raise the question: Should not the colonials be expected to assume some definite part of the cost of this? In view of the fact that . . . they were in a position to do so . . . [and] that the stability of these outlying possessions was a matter of greater concern and importance generally to them, by reason of their proximity, than to the people of the mother country three thousand miles away, the answer was in the affirmative. The reason for this is not hard to fathom. The nine years of war had involved Britons in tremendous expenditures. In spite of very heavy taxation during these years, the people were left saddled at the termination of hostilities with a national debt of unprecedented proportions for that day and age of over one hundred and forty million pounds. It was necessary not only to service and to retire this debt, in so far as was possible, but also to meet the ordinary demands of the civil government and to maintain the navy at a point of strength that . . . France and Spain would have no desire in the future to plan a war to recover their territorial losses. . . .

It may be noted that before the war the British budget had called for average annual expenditures of six and a half million pounds; between the years 1756 and 1766 these expenditures mounted to fourteen and a half million pounds a year on the average and from the latter date to 1775 ranged close to ten million pounds. As a result, the annual per capita tax in Great Britain, from 1763 to 1775, without considering local rates, was many times the average annual per capita tax in even those American colonies that made the greatest contribution to the Great War for the Empire, such as Massachusetts Bay and Connecticut . . . . The student of the history of the old British Empire, in fact, should accept with great reserve statements to the contrary—some of them quite irresponsible in nature—made by Americans during the heat of the controversy, with respect to the nature of the public burdens they were obliged to carry in the years preceding the outbreak of the Revolutionary War. . . . Well may John Adams have admitted in 1780 what was equally true in 1770: "America is not used to great taxes, and the people there are not yet disciplined to such enormous taxation as in England."

Assuming, as did the Grenville ministry in 1764, the justice of expecting the Americans to share in the cost of policing the new possessions in North America, the simplest and most obvious way, it might appear, to secure this contribution . . . was to request the colonial governments to make definite grants of funds. This was the requisition or quota system that had been employed in the course of the recent war. . . . Indeed, experience with this system in practice . . . had shown its weakness and utter unfairness. If it could not work equitably even in war time, could it be expected to work in peace? . . .

The plan of last resort to the ministry was therefore to ask Parliament to act. That Grenville, however, was aware that serious objections might be raised against any direct taxation of the colonials by the government of Great Britain is indicated by the caution with which he approached the solution of the problem of securing from America about a third of the total cost of its defense. The so-called Sugar Act first of all was passed at his request. This provided for import duties on certain West Indian and other products. Colonial import duties imposed by Parliament, at least since 1733, were no innovation. But the anticipated yield of these duties fell far short of the desired one hundred thousand pounds. He therefore . . . raised the question of a stamp duty but requested postponement of parliamentary action until the colonial governments had been consulted. The latter were thereupon requested to make any suggestions for ways of raising an American fund that might seem more proper to the people than such a tax. . . .

When—in view of the failure of the colonial governments to suggest any practicable, alternate plan . . . —Grenville finally urged in Parliament the passage of an American stamp bill, he acted on an unwarranted assumption. This assumption was—in paraphrasing the minister's remarks to the colonial agents in 1765—that opposition to stamp taxes, for the specific purpose in mind, would disappear in America both in light of the benefits such provision would bring to colonials in general and by reason of the plain justice of the measure itself; and that, in place of opposition, an atmosphere of mutual good-will would be generated by a growing recognition on the part of Americans that they could trust the benevolence of the mother country to act with fairness to all within the empire. Instead, with the news of the passage of the act, cries of British tyranny and impending slavery soon resounded throughout the entire eastern Atlantic American seaboard. . . .

But the Stamp Act was not the sole object of attack by colonials. To many of them not only the Sugar Act of 1764 but the whole English pre-war trade and navigation system was equally, if not actually more, obnoxious. Indeed, the unusual energy displayed by the navy and the customs officials . . . generated a degree of antagonism against the whole body of late seventeenth- and early eighteenth-century restrictions on commercial intercourse such as never had previously existed. It is not without significance that the greatest acts of terrorism and destruction during the great riot of August 1765 in Boston were directed not against the Massachusetts Bay stamp distributor but against those officials responsible for encouraging and supporting the enforcement, during the late war, of the various trade acts passed long before its beginning in 1754. The hatred also of the Rhode Island merchants, as a group, against the restrictions of the navigation system as well as against the Sugar Act of 1764, remained constant. Moreover, in December 1766 most of the New York merchants, over two hundred in number, showed their repugnance to the way that this system was functioning by a strongly worded petition to the House of Commons in which they enumerated an impressive list of grievances that they asked to be redressed. . . .

Nevertheless, the determination of the government . . . to enforce it now much more effectively than had been done before 1754, and to that end in 1767 to pass appropriate legislation . . . so that public officials in America might be held to greater accountability when paid their salaries by the Crown, could have only one result: the combined resistance of those, on the one hand, opposed to any type of taxation that Parliament might apply to America and of those, on the other, desiring to free the colonies of hampering trade restrictions. . . .

In accounting for the radical change in attitude of many leading colonials between the years 1754 and 1774 respecting the nature of the constitution of the empire, surely among the factors that must be weighed was the truly overwhelming victory achieved in the Great War for the Empire. This victory not only freed colonials for the first time in the history of the English-speaking people in the New World from dread of the French, their Indian allies, and the Spaniards, but, what is of equal significance, opened up to them the prospect, if given freedom of action, of a vast growth of power and wealth with an amazing westward expansion. Indeed, it is abundantly clear that a continued subordination of the colonies to the government of Great Britain was no longer considered an asset in the eyes of many Americans by 1774, as it had been so judged by them to be in 1754, but rather an onerous liability. What, pray tell, had the debt-ridden mother country to offer in 1774 to the now geographically secure, politically mature, prosperous, dynamic, and self-reliant offspring along the Atlantic seaboard, except the dubious opportunity of accepting new, as well as retaining old, burdens? . . .

At this point the question must be frankly faced: If France had won the war decisively and thereby consolidated her position and perfected her claims . . . , is it at all likely that colonials would have made so fundamental a constitutional issue of the extension to them of the principle of the British stamp tax? Would they have resisted such a tax . . . at a time when they were faced on their highly restricted borders by a militant, victorious enemy having at its command thousands of ferocious redskins? Again, accepting the fact of Britain's victory, is it not reasonable to believe that, had Great Britain at the close of the triumphant war left Canada to France and carefully limited her territorial demands in North America to those comparatively modest objectives that she had in mind at its beginning, there would have been no very powerful movement within the foreseeable future toward complete colonial autonomy—not to mention American independence? Would not Americans have continued to feel the need as in the past to rely for their safety and welfare upon British sea power and British land power, as well as upon British resources generally? In other words, was Governor Thomas Hutchinson of Massachusetts Bay far mistaken when, in analyzing the American situation late in 1773, he affirmed in writing to the Earl of Dartmouth:

"Before the peace [of 1763] I thought nothing so much to be desired as the cession of Canada. I am now convinced that if it had remained to the French none of the spirit of opposition to the Mother Country would have yet appeared & I think the effects of it [that is, the cession of Canada] worse than all we had to fear from the French or Indians."

In conclusion, it may be said that it would be idle to deny that most colonials in the eighteenth century at one time or another felt strongly the desire for freedom of action in a wider variety of ways than was legally permitted before 1754. Indeed, one can readily uncover these strong impulses even in the early part of the seventeenth century. Yet Americans were, by and large, realists, as were the British, and under the functioning of the imperial system from, let us say, 1650 to 1750 great mutual advantages were enjoyed, with a fair division, taking everything into consideration, of the financial burdens necessary to support the system. However, the mounting Anglo-French rivalry in North America from 1750 onward, the outbreak of hostilities in 1754, and the subsequent nine years of fighting destroyed the old equilibrium, leaving the colonials after 1760 in a highly favored position in comparison with the taxpayers of Great Britain. Attempts on the part of the Crown and Parliament to restore by statute the old balance led directly to the American constitutional crisis, out of which came the Revolutionary War and the establishment of American independence. Such, ironically, was the aftermath of the Great War for the Empire, a war that Britons believed, as the Earl of Shelburne affirmed in 1762 in Parliament, was begun for the "security of the British colonies in N. America."

Agitators and Propagandists

Learned and detailed writings on British mercantilism and American colonialism add greatly to knowledge of the Revolutionary period, but they do not always reflect the real spirit of the conflict. What aroused the violent passions in such patriots as Tom Paine, Samuel Adams, and the Sons of Liberty, those stalwart heroes of traditional history? Is it not possible to have abuses without resorting to revolution? History is full of such instances. Suppose the American people had been successful in avoiding armed conflict with England. Is it likely that the colonies might have taken the line of development followed by Canada toward independence without war?

A continued unrest often produces agitators and leaders who are not in themselves the cause of a revolutionary movement, but merely its instruments. Some great religious and political revolts resulted from the activities of small, fanatical groups. In almost every armed revolution, the boiler was heated by someone who kept it hot until it exploded. A few riots and unruly demonstrations, seemingly spontaneous, helped, especially when they were well publicized.

The American Revolution also had its firebrands, its riots, its committees, and its communications network. Tom Paine, who came to

America in 1774, was one of the greatest propagandists for the Revolution. His pamphlet, *Common Sense,* first published in 1776, enabled the people to see independence as a reality, and copies of the pamphlet sold by the hundreds of thousands throughout the colonies.

Samuel Adams also had a key role in stirring up the people. He was a born intriguer and the chief organizer among Massachusetts towns of the committees of correspondence. By the time of the Declaration of Independence, Sam Adams was regarded as the leading revolutionist in America, and the man whom one Tory called "that Machiavel of Chaos." Unlike his cousin John Adams, who was a great architect of government, Sam Adams was an expert at overthrowing them. He and his cohorts undoubtedly played a significant part in sparking the revolt.

Although no major school of historians has emphasized the importance of propagandists and agitators in precipitating the Revolution, two books appeared which argued for it convincingly. In *Propaganda and the American Revolution, 1763-1783,* published in 1941, Philip Davidson asserted that the American Revolution did not happen by chance but as the result of a conscious, systematic effort of an aggressive minority. Leaders and agitators of the Sam Adams type in all the colonies used propaganda effectively, spreading it through newspapers, broadsides, pictures, poems, songs, plays, public addresses, sermons, and demonstrations. Davidson said, "Without their work independence would not have been declared in 1776 nor recognized in 1783."

The second book is John C. Miller's *Sam Adams, Pioneer in Propaganda,* from which the excerpt in this Problem is taken. Centering on Adams' particular contributions, Miller's stirring account captures the excitement of the era.

As you read about Sam Adams' activities, consider the following questions:

1 The word *propaganda* is defined as systematic efforts to spread opinions and beliefs. Is the use of propaganda necessarily wrong?

2 Was Adams more an agitator than a propagandist? In what sort of activities did he achieve the greatest success?

3 Without Sam Adams and his counterparts in every hamlet and town in America, do you think there would have been an armed conflict? a revolution of any kind?

4 What seems to be Miller's attitude toward the revolutionary character of rural Americans?

5 Would the people in the outlying villages have joined Adams' forces without propaganda pressures?

"TRULY THE MAN OF THE REVOLUTION"

Sam Adams was a pioneer propagandist, but the techniques and psychology of persuasion he employed show him to be an expert. It was Thomas Jefferson who said he was "truly the Man of the Revolution." ☐ John C. Miller, *Sam Adams, Pioneer in Propaganda,* pp. 51–52, 61–63, 82–83, 85–86, 112–113, 137–139, 178, 180, 261–264, 269–272, 276, 291–296. Boston: Little, Brown & Company. Copyright © 1936 by John C. Miller.

Within a year of the passage of the Stamp Act by the British House of Commons, the American colonies were covered with Societies whose purpose was to nullify the act. The members of these clubs called themselves "Sons of Liberty"—a name derived from Isaac Barré's speech in Parliament in behalf of the colonies during the Stamp Act debate. By forming military alliances between the colonies, driving out the stamp masters and burning the stamps, the Sons of Liberty prevented the execution of the Stamp Act and usurped much of the real power of government in America. During the course of the Revolution they assumed many different names, but whether they called themselves committees of correspondence, committees of safety, or "true-born Whigs," the Sons of Liberty of 1765 were the radicals who led the colonies into revolution against the mother country.

When news of the Stamp Act reached the colonies, these patriotic societies spread rapidly over America. "The whole continent," George Bancroft said, "rang with the cheering name of the Sons of Liberty." But not all of the clubs that called themselves Sons of Liberty were founded spontaneously to resist the Stamp Act. Many had been in existence for years and had been created with no thought of resisting the "tyranny" of the mother country: their purpose was rather to combat the colonial aristocracy and give the unprivileged class a share of political power. . . .

The Boston Sons of Liberty, led by Sam Adams, boasted some of the most fiery, unruly Whigs on the continent. They were recruited largely from the wharfingers, artisans and shipyard workers of North Boston. . . . Although many wealthy merchants were known as Sons of Liberty and made an impressive show with their chariots in parades and celebrations, most of them were patriots out of prudence: when Boston swarmed with patriot mobs, it was well to be known as a Son of Liberty. The true Sons of Liberty—those who controlled the mobs and Boston elections—were a small group of politicians from the Caucus Club who met in a counting room on the second floor of Chase and Speakman's distillery. This building stood in Hanover Square near the Tree of Liberty—a huge oak that had been planted, it was significantly pointed out, in 1646, three years before the execution of Charles I. Tories always believed it important that the Liberty Boys had their meeting place conveniently near a liquor supply such as that afforded by Chase and Speakman's distillery, since it was supposed their courage arose chiefly "from the steams of their poisonous rum." . . .

Virginia led the way in constitutional protest against the Stamp Act, but Massachusetts was foremost in riots. In the summer of 1765, Sam Adams determined to terrorize Andrew Oliver, [Lieutenant Governor] Thomas Hutchinson's brother-in-law, who had been appointed stamp master of Massachusetts Bay, into resigning office in order that the stamps could not be distributed in the colony. During the night of August 14, 1765, the "Loyall Nine," probably acting under orders from Sam Adams, hung an effigy of Oliver on Liberty Tree, where it was found the next morning by the astonished citizens. The Crown officers at first supposed it was merely a boyish prank, but when the sheriff reported he could not take down the effigy without risking his life, they began to suspect that this was not altogether child's play. When one of the spectators at Liberty Tree asked Sam Adams, who was standing under the tree peering up at the effigy, who it was, Adams answered that "he did not know—he could not tell—he wanted to enquire." Nevertheless, it soon became clear that Sam Adams and the Sons of Liberty planned an eventful evening for Boston: the crowds that gathered on street corners throughout the afternoon grew by nightfall into a large mob that paraded around the Town House where the governor and Council were sitting, giving "three huzzas by way of Defiance" as it passed. After destroying a building recently erected near the water front by Oliver, which was believed to be designed as a stamp headquarters, the mob marched to Oliver's house and beheaded his effigy. After giving the stamp master this significant foretaste of what he might expect at their hands, the rioters built a huge bonfire on Fort Hill. The demonstration was now thought to be over, and the gentlemen and "persons of character" who had been in the mob to keep order, "disguised with trousers & Jackets," went home for the night, leaving the rest of the rioters around the fire. But a large number of the mob felt they had spent a very tame evening: therefore, no sooner were the gentlemen rioters out of sight than they rushed down Fort Hill to Oliver's house, led by Andrew Mackintosh, a cobbler and chief of the South End mob. After shattering Oliver's windowpanes with a hail of brickbats, several ruffians broke into the house and began to search for the stamp master, swearing they would kill him if he fell into their hands. Governor Bernard could do nothing to restore order: when he called for his drummers to beat the alarm, he was told they were in the mob. Had not Hutchinson already persuaded Oliver to get out of harm's way, he probably would have been roughly handled indeed during the "furious Onset." But, although Oliver escaped unhurt, the riot accomplished its chief purpose, for the next day he promised to resign as stamp master.

The fourteenth of August, the day on which this riot took place, was celebrated in New England for many years to commemorate "the happy Day, on which Liberty arose from a long Slumber." Sam Adams said it "ought to be for ever remembered in America" because "the People shouted; and their shout was heard to the distant end of this Continent." . . .

The Stamp Act had brought Sam Adams out of obscurity and placed him in the General Court [or legislative body] where he was to remain for the next decade despite the Tories' best efforts to dislodge him. In 1764, Adams [had] seemed destined to remain unknown except, perhaps, for the brief notoriety he had received for embezzling public funds. By 1766, when the Stamp Act was repealed, he had become one of the most important figures in Massachusetts politics, second only to James Otis in popularity. Decidedly, it behooved the Tories to look closely at this man whose rapid rise threatened to destroy their influence in New England.

They saw a middle-aged man, already stricken with palsy, whose clothing was invariably rusty from long use. There was little arresting in his appearance and even to his friends he seemed merely a "plain, simple, decent citizen, of middling stature, dress and manners," who lived frugally and took great pride in his poverty. Tories always professed to see in Adams's face strong traces of the "Malignity" of his heart. An American painter who knew him well is said to have remarked that "if he wished to draw the Picture of the Devil . . . he would get Sam Adams to sit for him." It is singular that this resemblance to Satan which his enemies found so striking does not appear in any of Adams's portraits. It cannot be said that Tory painters did not have opportunity to expose Adams's diabolical qualities, for his best-known portrait is by John Singleton Copley, the greatest of Tory artists, but there is no sign of the cloven hoof in Copley's study of Adams . . . .

One of Sam Adams's most effective ways of arousing patriotic fervor in New England was to appeal to the example of the early Puritans who had lived frugally, loved their liberties, hated the devil, and looked with no friendly eye upon the British government. He always said his purpose was to revive the "ancestorial Spirit of Liberty" in the people rather than to indoctrinate them with newfangled revolutionary principles. Like many other leaders who have precipitated great changes, he regarded himself not as an innovator but as a restorer of the past. When the patriot cause seemed blackest and hardship began to turn the citizens from Whig principles, Adams rallied his followers by reminding them of the sufferings their ancestors had undergone to establish liberty in the New World. He firmly believed that New Englanders' best security against British tyranny was the Puritan spirit, which, although sadly weakened in the course of a century, might again be made a bulwark of colonial liberty. . . .

Massachusetts Whigs had fallen upon evil days [after 1766], but Sam Adams's skill in staging patriotic parades, feasts, and celebrations served to conceal most evidence of the patriot decline. He believed men were ruled by their emotions rather than by their reason, and he knew that a display of fireworks on the Boston Common or parades of marching Sons of Liberty were far more effective ways of arousing popular enthusiasm than dry constitutional arguments. Unquestionably, he was a master of stagecraft, deeply versed in the art of swaying the popular mind. The Sons of Liberty celebrated the repeal of the Stamp Act with "such illuminations, bonfires, pyramids, obelisks, such grand exhibitions and such fireworks as were never before seen in America." Effigies of popular enemies were used to inflame the people's passion; cartoons exhibiting in easily understood form the wickedness of the Tories and mother country were passed from hand to hand; stirring phrases were coined and spread among the common people with greater effect than whole volumes of political reasoning; and Whig newspapers carried the radicalism of the seaboard towns to every corner of the province. John Adams, too, saw the importance of Whig parades, fireworks, and propaganda: "Otis and Adams are politic in promoting these festivals," he wrote, "for they tinge the minds of people; they impregnate them with the sentiments of liberty; they render the people fond of their leaders in the cause, and averse and bitter against all opposers." The Tories, on the other hand, knew nothing of influencing the common people; instead of attempting to wean them from Sam Adams, they merely sneered at them as "the rabble" or "the scum." The fatal error made by Massachusetts conservatives during the revolutionary period was their failure to recognize the importance of the common people in the coming struggle between mother country and colonies. . . .

The cornerstone of Sam Adams's policy was to put New England in leading strings to Boston and make farmers as zealous Sons of Liberty as were the North End mechanics and shipyard workers. He knew that the metropolis could not oppose Parliament single-handed and that before Massachusetts could assume the leadership of the American colonies against Great Britain, yeomen must learn to look upon Boston as a bulwark of their liberties. Adams hoped to see town and country sink their differences when confronted by British tyranny. . . .

. . . Through the *Boston Gazette*—printed by those "Trumpeters of Sedition," Edes and Gill—he continually drenched the country with propaganda. He filled its columns with such dire prophecies of disaster and terrifying descriptions of "horred slavery" at the hands of British overlords that many yeomen were transformed into fiery Whigs. It was said of this journal that if its readers were "not in the temper of the writer at the time of publication, yet it is looked upon as the *oracle,* and they soon bring their temper to it." Furthermore, it made vastly more exciting reading than did the dull conservative newspapers that attempted to keep the country people loyal to King and Parliament; indeed, Sam Adams's journalism was so lively that the *Gazette* became practically the only newspaper read outside of Boston. Although it was packed with sedition and libel, it could not be suppressed by the Crown officers; when Hutchinson attempted to induce the Suffolk Grand Jury to indict the author of a particularly "blasphemous Abuse of Kingly Government," Sam Adams brought so much pressure to bear upon the jury that the indictment was promptly quashed. During the Stamp Act, Tories had received a bitter taste of the power of the patriot press. The Stamp Act riots in Boston were so glorified by Sam Adams in the *Gazette* that rural patriots were sorely troubled because no mobs sprang up in rural New England to harry the Tories. Upcountry Whigs asked themselves "ye Reason *we* could do nothing when Such Great Things were done at Boston." Countrymen who bore a grudge against the local squire imitated Sam Adams by threatening to get up a mob, pull down the house, and give the "aristocrat" a coat of tar and feathers. Several gangs of Sons of Liberty, with an eye toward making patriotism profitable, raided the houses of their creditors and wiped out their debts by tearing up the ledgers and account books. . . .

Early in the spring of 1770 the situation in Boston passed entirely out of the control of the peace officers. Sam Adams's "Mohawks" brawled with redcoats in taverns and back alleys while the ropewalkers [workers in a rope-making establishment] picked quarrels with the Twenty-ninth Regiment—those guardians of law and order whose bad tempers were the terror of sober citizens whether Whig or Tory. Then, in March 1770, an incident occurred which led directly to the Boston Massacre. Samuel Gray, one of the hardiest brawlers employed at Gray's ropewalk in Boston, asked a soldier of the Twenty-ninth Regiment if he wanted a job. When the man answered that he did, Gray said he had a privy that needed cleaning. This insult provoked an immediate fight between the soldiers and ropewalkers, but no serious clash took place until their pent-up animosity burst forth on March 5, 1770. . . . [At nine o'clock that evening a mob pressured a soldier.

He called for help from the main guard, and during the commotion that followed someone fired into the mob, killing three and fatally wounding two.]

Sam Adams lost no time in making the most of the "Bloody Work in King's Street." The day after the Massacre, the town meeting was called in Faneuil Hall, where Adams made such a rousing speech from the rostrum that his hearers declared it was "enough to fire any heart with a desire to become a patriot." Having thrown the citizens into this bristling frame of mind, Adams demanded the immediate withdrawal of the British troops from Boston. This, the townspeople agreed, was the only way to prevent further "blood and carnage." Adams thereupon placed himself and Hancock at the head of a town committee and marched to the Town House overlooking the scene of the Massacre, where, in the Council chamber hung with the portraits of Charles II and James II and "little miserable likenesses" of the Puritan magistrates, Adams laid his demands before the Council. At the head of the Council table sat Lieutenant Governor Hutchinson; at his right, Colonel Dalrymple, commander in chief of His Majesty's forces in Boston; and around the table were seated twenty-eight councilors . . . . Standing before these dignitaries as spokesman for the citizens of Boston, Adams described the "dangerous, ruinous, and fatal effects of standing armies in populous cities in time of peace," the hatred of New Englanders toward the troops who had spilled patriot blood, and repeated the resolves of the Boston town meeting demanding the immediate removal of the soldiers from the metropolis. Hutchinson answered that since he had no authority over the King's troops nothing could be done until he had consulted the home government. But Adams was not to be put off so easily; he instantly appealed to the Massachusetts charter by which Hutchinson was constituted commander in chief of all the military and naval forces within the province. . . . Unless the metropolis were cleared of redcoats, Adams warned, there would be more bloody work in Boston—this time with the King's troops as the victims. Fifteen thousand fighting men, he exclaimed, were ready to pour into Boston to take revenge upon the soldiers. Dalrymple needed little persuasion: he was well aware that he could not defend his position against the New England militia with the four hundred men he could bring into the field; and he had no desire to risk a disgraceful rout at the hands of farmers and Boston Sons of Liberty. . . . The danger of defying the people was too great; before nightfall, Hutchinson struck his colors and Bostonians were promised the speedy removal of . . . [the] regiments. . . .

In 1772, while Adams was making political capital out of Hutchinson's pension [Hutchinson had been made Governor and was to receive his salary from the British government instead of from Massachusetts] a rumor reached Boston that the judges of the Massachusetts superior court were likewise to be made independent of the legislature for their support. . . .

The rumor . . . gave Adams the opportunity he had long been waiting. It was true that he had only a rumor to work upon, but Adams had the gift of dressing hearsay and tavern gossip into fact in the pages of the of the *Boston Gazette*. . . .

Sam Adams's home thrust at British tyranny was the establishment of the committees of correspondence. Corresponding committees had been used by American patriots from the beginning of the controversy with the mother country: merchants' corresponding committees had organized resistance to the Sugar Act of 1764 and the Sons of Liberty had covered the colonies with a network of societies whose circular letters and secret correspondence were one of the most striking manifestations of colonial unity during the Stamp Act period. . . . The first step in this ambitious undertaking was to link the towns of Massachusetts Bay together so closely that they would present a solid "phalanx" to the British government—"a band of brothers, which no force can break, no enemy destroy." Once Adams's radical followers— under the name of committees of correspondence—were in power in every Massachusetts town, the whole colony would act in concert with Boston and the rural representatives would be sent down to the General Court with instructions to join the metropolis in whatever measures it took to oppose the mother country. With committees of correspondence ruling the province there would be little danger of the country deserting Boston in an emergency. Such union between town and country would exhilarate the Whig morale, which, since the failure of patriot policies after the Massacre, had reached a low ebb. . . .

Yet few Whigs agreed with Sam Adams that the iron was sufficiently hot to strike such a heavy blow at British authority in Massachusetts. Almost single-handed, and against the opposition of most of his lieutenants, Adams brought forth the Boston committee of correspondence and thereby hatched the "foulest, subtlest, and most venomous serpent ever issued from the egg of sedition." . . .

The committees of correspondence mark the rejuvenation of the Whig Party in the American colonies and the reappearance of Sam Adams as a serious menace to the stability of the British Empire. As Adams himself said, the committees diverted the people's attention from "picking up pins, and directed their Views to great objects"—with the result that politics again became the besetting passion of New Englanders and "the Genius of Liberty" was once more "Roused after a Languor if not profound Sleep."

Sam Adams was once more regarded as the watchdog of New England's liberties, alert to all British "Schemes to Subvert our happy Constitution." With Adams on the lookout, the Boston committee never lacked alarming rumors of impending British tyranny which, when sent over the network of corresponding committees, kept New Englanders constantly on edge for their liberties. As soon as the local committee received word from Boston of the plots being hatched by British ministers against colonial freedom, the town meeting was called and instructions were rushed to the representatives in the General Court to uphold Sam Adams' policies against the mother country. For the benefit of backward towns, the Boston committee sent out circular letters containing political doctrines which Adams judged proper for rural patriots. The answers that poured into Boston from the interior were highly gratifying to Sam Adams, who had gambled everything on the hope that the rural districts would again become a hotbed of Whiggery. . . .

But while Adams thus educated New Englanders in "Boston principles" he was careful to lead the country people to believe that instead of being led by Boston they themselves were in reality the leaders. Bostonians had no wish, said Adams, to "obtrude *their* Opinions upon their Fellow-Countrymen," and he flattered the village Hampdens by assuring them that their "resolution to oppose Tyranny in all its forms is worthy the Imitation of this Metropolis." In his letters to rural patriots he skillfully soothed their distrust of the metropolis and overcame their unwillingness to be led by town folk into a quarrel with the mother country. He always spoke of back-country Whigs as his "sensible Brethren in the Country" or as his "worthy & much esteemed Brethren." Indeed, if Sam Adams were to be believed, the Boston Sons of Liberty were merely responding to pressure from the country people in provoking controversy with Great Britain. . . .

. . . The committees of correspondence that made the American Revolution possible were the town committees dominated by local "Sam Adamses" who were in close touch with Boston and other centres of radicalism. These committees owed their origin to Sam Adams rather than to the Virginia Whigs. Without their aid it is doubtful if the first Continental Congress would have been held in 1774 and the revolutionary movement in the colonies brought to its fruition in the Declaration of Independence. They made possible the domination of a great part of British America by cliques of radical patriots who looked to Sam Adams for leadership against the mother country. These committees were a direct outgrowth of the intercolonial unity that had been seen in the military alliances and corresponding committees of the Sons of Liberty during the Stamp Act. After 1774, the colonies fairly bristled with hot-tempered Liberty Boys, who, instead of calling themselves Sons of Liberty, were now known as the committees of correspondence. But under whatever name these patriots worked, their purpose remained the same: to defend colonial liberty with arms rather than submit to British "tyranny." . . .

Because Sam Adams and other leaders of the American Revolution have handed down to posterity self-portraits in which they exhibit themselves as patient, peace-loving men driven to rebellion by intolerable British tyranny, the fact that they themselves made repeated aggressions upon the British government and did much to precipitate the Revolution is often overlooked. After the Massachusetts Convention of 1768, Sam Adams deliberately set out to provoke crises that would lead to the separation of mother country and colonies. He had scored his most notable success in the Boston Massacre . . . . A far greater triumph was the Boston Tea Party, which, by precipitating the American Revolution, deserves to rank as the masterpiece of Sam Adams's efforts to create an unbridgeable gap between Great Britain and her American provinces. . . .

The menace of East India tea revealed what a powerful revolutionary machine Sam Adams had created in the Boston committee of correspondence. The committee took complete charge in Boston and directed the patriots' activities, which culminated in the destruction of the tea. By means of the committees of correspondence, Adams kept the people in a state of feverish excitement. . . .

The destruction of the tea struck Boston patriot leaders as the only effective solution of the deadlock that Sam Adams had created . . . . There was in Boston a large body of men ready for any violence: several hundred "veteran Sons of Liberty," it was said, were enrolled in the metropolis to destroy the tea or "perish in the Attempt." Moreover, the British force in the vicinity was not likely to give trouble: only one regiment of royal troops was in Castle William, and the townspeople had no fears of the British fleet in the harbor because they believed that the admiral "might as well hang himself, as burn the town." . . .

. . . On the afternoon of December 16, several thousand people crowded into the Old South Meetinghouse to demand that Rotch, one of the owners of the tea ships, make a last effort to secure a clearance from Hutchinson. The candles were being lighted when Rotch returned to the Old South with Hutchinson's refusal. In the gathering dusk, Sam Adams arose and solemnly declared that "this meeting can do nothing further to save the country". His words were the signal for a wild war whoop from the galleries and the street outside the meetinghouse where several hundred "Mohawks," who had been fortifying themselves with punch and putting the finishing touches on their Indian make-up at Edes and Gill's printing shop, broke from the crowd and headed for the water front closely followed by a mob of spectators. As this howling procession approached the water front there was such an uproar that "you'd thought the inhabitants of the infernal regions had broke loose." Most of the "Narragansett Indians" were Adams's followers from the North End—shipyard workers, artisans, and ship masters—decked out in war paint and feathers. Once aboard the tea ships, the braves worked quickly, and within a few moments three hundred and forty-two chests of the finest tea that ever tempted New Englanders' palates, pocketbooks, and patriotism were at the bottom of Boston Harbor.

After the Tea Party, Sam Adams and the Boston Whigs were in "a perfect Jubillee." For, as Hutchinson said, it was "the boldest stroke which had yet been struck in America" and fully restored Boston to the leadership of the American colonies. . . .

Thus, by its achievement in forcing the British government's hand in the colonies and rallying colonial radicals to Boston's defense, the Tea Party might well be regarded as a crossing of the Rubicon which left Sam Adams the desperate alternative of "Neck or Nothing." It was a headlong plunge toward revolt which set free the forces, long gathering in America, that led to war between the mother country and colonies. The British government could not overlook the insult it had received at the hands of Sam Adams and his "Mohawks"; but British statesmen were utterly unaware of the true strength of the revolutionary movement in America. And it was clear that upon their decision hung "the fate of a great empire."

The Revolutionary War:
A Survey

This unit has presented some of the major interpretations of the origins of the American Revolution: the nationalist tradition, the economic interpretation, the ideas of the imperial school, and the views of scholars who stress the role of agitators and propagandists.

A point of view which has reëmerged emphasizes colonial desire for home rule and proper treatment under British constitutional principles. In 1960 Page Smith called attention to David Ramsay, a historian who had received relatively little recognition. Ramsay was a doctor in South Carolina, a patriot who took part in the Revolution, and a delegate to the Continental Congress. Smith believed Ramsay's *History of the American Revolution,* published in 1793, to be the best account of the causes of the Revolutionary War.

Ramsay, like all the first generation historians, regarded mercantilism as a moderate system in which the good outweighed the evil. As contributing causes of the war, he mentioned the Puritan and Protestant traditions of opposition to arbitrary authority, the feebleness of British rule in America, and the growing belief among Americans that their assemblies bore the same relationship to them that Parliament did to Englishmen. Above all, Ramsay emphasized the Stamp Act crisis as crucial and argued that resistance to the act was not primarily economic but was based on a political principle.

A return to this idea appeared in 1953 in *The Stamp Act Crisis,* which Edmund S. Morgan wrote with his wife Helen M. Morgan. Morgan hinged his argument, as Ramsay did, on the decisive importance of the Stamp Act. It is interesting that a historian, whose specialty is colonial history, should offer in the 1950's an interpretation so similar to one presented 160 years ago. Does this weaken the argument that historical objectivity is achieved only by those writers sufficiently separated in time from the actual events? Present-day students have an excellent opportunity to study varying interpretations in such a summary as that offered in the selection written by Edmund S. Morgan. From these differing perspectives the student may develop insights and make discoveries which will help him in formulating his own conclusions. As you read, consider these questions:

1   What interpretations described in the Morgan selection would you have included in place of any, or all, of the first four readings in this unit? Why?

2   Do you agree with some of the historians cited in this selection that the causes of the American Revolution stemmed mainly from internal conflicts among the colonists rather than from external causes?

3   Considering the fact that Morgan has his own interpretation, do you feel that he has given a balanced treatment to the various approaches of other historians?

4   If, as Morgan says, historians still "do not fully know" what the Revolution was, what stands in the way of achieving this goal?

5   Is historical truth always the same, or does it change relative to the time in which the history is written?

WHAT WAS THE AMERICAN REVOLUTION?

Edmund S. Morgan reviews the contributions of nineteenth- and twentieth-century writers in seeking an answer to this question. ☐ Edmund S. Morgan, *The American Revolution, A Review of Changing Interpretations,* pp. 1–15, 18. Washington, D.C.: Service Center for Teachers of History. Copyright © 1958 by the American Historical Association.

Americans who lived from 1763 to 1789 witnessed the most remarkable transformation in our history, from empire to republic, from colony to state, from multiplicity to union. Events moved so rapidly in those years that we do not hesitate to use the word "revolution" in talking about them. But everyone who has studied them knows how hard it is to decide what was revolutionary and what was not. What was old and what was new? What *was* the American Revolution?

Until the present century the answer most often given to this question was the one formulated by George Bancroft, the first great historian to deal with it (*History of the United States,* 10 vols., 1834–74) . . . .

Bancroft tended to look upon any exertion of English authority in America as a usurpation. He even labelled his chapter on the exploration of Virginia in the sixteenth century with the audacious title, "England takes possession of the United States." English mercantilism, expressed in the Navigation Acts, seemed to him almost an infringement of United States sovereignty, something that Andrew Jackson would never have put up with. By the time one has read through Bancroft's early volumes, the Revolution comes as no surprise. George III is only the last of a bad lot, while the Americans of 1776 are a line of men who first resisted tyranny under the Stuarts.

It is easy today to discover the weaknesses in Bancroft. For him everything was black or white. He abused quotations shamelessly. He chopped truths in half and sometimes offered up the smaller part. But we will err more seriously than he if we disregard him. He did not write in ignorance. Probably no one else has known the original sources for the Revolutionary period as well as he, and he knew them when only a small portion had found their way into print. Even today anyone who has worked through the unpublished Revolutionary manuscripts in some of our great repositories will find it instructive to go to Bancroft and see evidence of his familiarity with them. He simplified, yes, but simplification is the business of the historian; and though he has been proved wrong at many points, no one else has yet been able to bend his bow. No one has yet rewritten the history of the Revolution on the grand scale.

It is perhaps no coincidence that the one historian who came closest to it was an Englishman writing with a similar animus against George III and a similar fondness for old-fashioned political liberty. Sir George Otto Trevelyan was a nineteenth-century Whig in search of his Party's eighteenth-century forbears. He found them, as he thought, among the men who opposed George III during the disastrous ministry of Lord North. His four volumes on *The American Revolution* (1898–1907) show a small band of dedicated men, the Rockingham Whigs, arrayed against a power-hungry king and a corrupt horde of place-hunters. The Whigs do their best to halt the drive toward tyranny, but the king and his cohorts overpower them, until American success and royal failure bring a new dispensation to British politics. . . .

Even before Trevelyan finished telling his story, a new school of historians had begun to re-examine the assumptions upon which he and Bancroft proceeded. Most of these historians did not directly approach the Revolution itself. Instead, they fastened upon the earlier history of the colonies, which for Bancroft had exhibited the same forces that produced the Revolution. Was the old British Empire, they asked, so bad a thing as Bancroft implied? Were the restrictions placed on the colonists unfair? To both these questions they returned a resounding "No."

The first effective spokesman of this "imperial" school of history was George Louis Beer, a New York tobacco merchant, who had studied history at Columbia. . . . In 1907 he produced his *British Colonial Policy 1754–1765*, which demonstrated that the behavior of the American colonists during the Seven Years' War was far from commendable, while that of Great Britain was constructive and responsible. The colonists, he thought, offered little loyalty and no gratitude to the country which protected them from the French and Spanish. Once the French menace was destroyed, they moved swiftly toward independence, not in order to preserve civil or political liberty, but because they had nothing further to gain by remaining in the empire. . . .

Beer's work, in spite of his strong attachment to Anglo-American union, was based on careful scholarship. Both his scrupulousness as a scholar and much of his point of view were carried on by the great colonial historian, Charles McLean Andrews. Andrews, like Beer, gave his attention principally to the period before the Revolution. He trained a generation of scholars to look at colonial history as imperial history. . . . And the students who traversed colonial history under Andrews' guidance arrived at the Revolution with a sympathetic understanding of the problems with which British administrators had to wrestle. The Navigation Acts appeared no longer to be an instrument of economic oppression but rather a sensible means of giving England a return for the protection she furnished to the colonists. The Admiralty Courts ceased to be a tool of tyranny and became useful devices for keeping trade and commerce flowing. . . .

Andrews' students have continued the study of British policy, and among other notable studies they have produced is Leonard W. Labaree's *Royal Government in America* (1930), which discusses at length the friction between royal governors and colonial assemblies. It has remained for another of Andrews' students, Lawrence H. Gipson, to undertake a full-scale consideration, from the imperial point of view, of the events leading up to the Declaration of Independence. In a monumental study, still under way, of *The British Empire before the American Revolution* (1936—), Gipson surveyed the condition of the empire in 1750, not neglecting its eastern as well as its western outposts, and then began the long march toward 1776. In the eighth volume he reached the conclusion of the Seven Years' War, which in its imperial phase he renamed "The Great War for the Empire." His view of the conduct of Americans in this war was no higher than that of Beer. The war, as Professor Gipson sees it, was won primarily by English money and English blood, both of which were spilt freely in America. . . .

In stressing the inconstancy of colonial arguments against taxation, Professor Gipson has claimed no more than several historians of American political ideas, none of whom falls properly within the imperial, or any other, school of interpretation. Carl Becker, in *The Declaration of Independence* (1922) discussed with his usual felicity the American expression of eighteenth-century political ideas. He showed the colonists moving through a series of preliminary stages before they reached a total denial of Parliament's authority. At the time of the Stamp Act, he maintained, they objected to internal taxes but admitted the validity of external ones. After Parliament took them at their word and levied the external Townshend duties, they shifted to a denial of all Parliamentary taxes but admitted that Parliament could regulate their trade. By the time of the First Continental Congress they were ready to refuse Parliament any authority over them at all.

Randolph G. Adams in *The Political Ideas of the American Revolution* (1922) traced the same progression. Adams was primarily interested in the conception of the British Empire expressed in the last stage of American opposition, that of an empire with several co-ordinate legislatures, linked only by allegiance to a common sovereign. This conception later proved fruitful in keeping the rest of Britain's empire together, and Adams praised the vision of the men who formulated it. But he readily agreed that it was inconsistent with the ideas expressed in the early years of opposition to Parliament. Even Charles Howard McIlwain, who argued in *The American Revolution: A Constitutional Interpretation* (1923) for the constitutional validity of this conception of empire, admitted that the colonists did not reach it until they had tried less valid ideas. (McIlwain's contention that the final colonial position was constitutionally valid is questioned by Robert L. Schuyler in *Parliament and the British Empire* [1929].)

The most recent detailed account of the development of Revolutionary political theory is Clinton Rossiter's *Seedtime of the Republic* (1953), which follows Bancroft in seeking the roots of American freedom deep in the colonial past. Rossiter, like Becker and Adams, is sympathetic with the Americans, but he too acknowledges that the Americans shifted their ground several times after the controversy began.

It would appear then, that Bancroft's story of English tyranny and American liberty has undergone revision. Historians of political thought have agreed that the Americans were inconsistent or wavering in their devotion to principles, and the imperial historians have found them selfish and narrow by comparison with their English masters. . . .

When we compare the new views held by historians of British politics, of the empire, and of political ideas, we find certain inconsistencies. . . . Until the new views are reconciled in a new synthesis, we can only speculate on what relative importance to assign them. One thing, however, is clear: they all demand that we re-examine the question as to why there should have been a revolution at all. If the Navigation Acts were fair, if Americans were not initially attached to any particular view of Parliament's authority, if George III was no tyrant, why should the colonists have sought independence? What, again, *was* the Revolution? If Bancroft's answer was wrong, what should we put in its place?

Historians have not neglected this question, and the answer that seems to have pleased them most, at least until recently, was that offered by Carl Becker. In his *History of Political Parties in the Province of New York, 1760–1776* (1909), Becker said that the politics of New York in the Revolutionary period revolved around two questions, home rule and who should rule at home. Everyone knew that the Revolution was fought to gain home rule, in other words, independence. Becker's statement, and the substance of his book, drew attention to a simultaneous conflict among the colonists themselves. . . .

. . . Succeeding historians have carried his interpretation somewhat further. Arthur Meier Schlesinger in *The Colonial Merchants and the American Revolution* (1918) examined the role of the merchants of all the colonies in the troubled twelve years preceding the Declaration of Independence. In the initial opposition to the Sugar Act and the Stamp Act he found the merchants playing a leading role. The Stamp Act riots, however, gave them pause. When the Townshend Acts were passed, they resorted again to nonimportation agreements but took a firm stand against violence. As the lower classes became enthusiastic about nonimportation, the merchants grew less so. After 1770 they did their best to keep the lower classes under control and to prevent outbreaks of hostility to England. Only when the Tea Act threatened to cut them out of the tea business did they again take the lead in opposing Britain. The results of their opposition were so catastrophic that many quickly drew back, but too late. Professor Schlesinger brought his story to a close with the coming of independence, but in a final chapter he looked ahead toward the war and the years just after it, to see the merchants and aristocrats still arrayed against the same lower classes who had come into prominence in the Revolutionary agitations.

Both Becker and Schlesinger were writing about particular developments during the Revolution, Becker about politics in New York, Schlesinger about merchants in all the colonies. J. Franklin Jameson undertook to view the entire Revolution as a democratic upheaval, beginning perhaps as a mere political protest against certain acts of Parliament, but fanning out in the same manner as the French and Russian Revolutions, to transform the whole society (*The American Revolution Considered as a Social Movement* [1926]). "The stream of revolution," said Jameson, "once started, could not be confined within narrow banks, but spread abroad upon the land" (p. 11). And he traced its outflowing in a multitude of social changes, all of them "tending in the direction of a levelling democracy" (p. 25). The abolition of the slave trade and of slavery in many states, the abolition of primogeniture and entail, the confiscation and dispersal of loyalists estates, the reduction in the property qualification for voting, the disestablishment of the Anglican Church—in these and similar developments Jameson saw the ultimate answer to the question of who should rule at home.

The social view of the Revolution, as expressed by Becker, Schlesinger, and Jameson, maximizes the conflicts among the colonists themselves. It thereby tends to minimize the struggle between the colonies and England. We see why the colonists disliked each other, but why they were so angry with England is less clearly revealed.

A possible answer is propaganda. Two important books have discussed the methods by which agitators and demagogues disseminated propaganda to create popular hostility against the mother country. In *Sam Adams: Pioneer in Propaganda* (1936), John Chester Miller showed how one man led Massachusetts through the events that precipitated revolt. In *Propaganda and the American Revolution* (1941), Philip Davidson showed how other agitators and groups of agitators played on popular passions in all the colonies. . . . There [is] . . . a feeling that the Revolution, so far as it was a movement for home rule, grew out of the efforts of agitators like Sam Adams and Patrick Henry, who magnified England's sins in order to gain their own particular ends.

This is scarcely a complete answer. But neither the imperial nor the social-economic historians, both of whom rely on it, have shown much interest in finding a better one. It has been suggested that the Revolution was the inevitable result of colonial economic growth; but such a thesis has not yet been demonstrated in any extended study of the period. The historians who stress economic and social forces have, in fact, been less concerned with the causes of colonial hostility to England than with the subsequent history of the social divisions which Becker and Schlesinger observed in the years before independence. What happened, they ask, to the old ruling class within the colonies? . . .

It is in this context that we must read Charles Beard's *An Economic Interpretation of the Constitution* (1913), one of the most influential books ever written on American history. Published shortly after Becker's study, Beard's book, though it did not touch upon the Revolution itself, probably did more than Becker's to persuade historians that the whole Revolutionary period must be viewed in terms of class conflict.

The heart of Beard's book is a person-by-person examination of the fifty-five members of the Constitutional Convention of 1787 (Beard anticipated Namier in this technique of historical investigation). On the basis of Treasury records Beard was able to show that most of these men held public securities which rose in value as a result of the new Constitution. By stiffening both the government and the credit of the United States they made their investments in its funds pay off. They may have operated on the assumption that what was good for them was good for the country, but Beard argues that they had invested in personal, as opposed to real, property, that they designed the Constitution to bolster the security of this kind of property, and that they were able to put it across only because a majority of the population did not vote. Thus the founding fathers from Beard's study appear as a talented group of capitalist speculators who succeed in bamboozling the common man into acceptance of a form of government that was calculated to benefit a few uncommon men.

It is not difficult to identify Beard's personal property-holders as the economic descendants, or perhaps the very same men (it was only eleven years from the Declaration of Independence to the Constitutional Convention) as Arthur Schlesinger's merchants or Carl Becker's New York aristocrats. If Beard's view was correct, it would seem that the aristocrats who lost control but not influence in 1776 regained full power in 1789. . . .

Thus from a variety of works we gain a consistent explanation of the entire period from 1763 to 1789. The dominant theme is that of class conflict, the question of who shall rule at home. In the period of agitation preceding independence the masses are aroused to action against a supposed British tyranny but discover some additional and more accessible native tyrannies to exercise their wrath against. With the coming of independence they manage to achieve many reforms in the interest of a broader democracy, but the conservative property-holders and capitalist speculators manage to hang on and finally gain the upper hand with the adoption of the Constitution.

This interpretation, constructed of several different pieces of research, has an attractive symmetry. It makes sense out of the whole period and even points the way to a similar interpretation of the rest of American history as the story of democratic aspirations against upper-class despotism. It looks forward to the Jeffersonian revolution of 1800, Jacksonian democracy, Populism, Progressivism, the New Deal, all embodiments of the spirit of '76, and to the Federalists, the Whigs, the post-Civil War Republicans, all representing resurgent aristocracy.

During the first four decades of the twentieth century, when Progressivism and the New Deal commanded the allegiance of most intellectuals, this interpretation was almost irresistible. Charles Beard's *Economic Interpretation of the Constitution* was itself a weapon of Progressivism, directed against a Supreme Court which wielded the Constitution as a club against social legislation. The forties and fifties have witnessed a change. We have the social legislation now [1958]; and we also have an . . . [unparalleled] prosperity. Perhaps because our own period does not display the lines of class conflict so clearly as did the earlier part of the century, we are able to see less of it in the Revolution than we had once supposed to be there. Or perhaps, after two generations of professional scholarship, we know enough now to form a more accurate appraisal. Whatever the reason, during the past fifteen years a number of studies have appeared that begin to alter the previous answers to the question of what the Revolution was.

One of the most important of the newer studies is Oliver M. Dickerson's *The Navigation Acts and the American Revolution* (1951). In the first part of this book the author demonstrates that the Americans did not object to the Navigation Acts or to the mercantilist policies they represented. In this view he continues the familiar attack of the imperial school of historians on Bancroft. In the second part of the book Professor Dickerson addresses himself to the question which so few recent historians have asked: why did the Americans revolt against England?

Professor Dickerson's answer is new. The heart of the trouble, he says, was the American Board of Customs Commissioners established at Boston in 1767. Before that year American customs officers reported directly to a Board of Commissioners in England. With the creation by the Townshend Acts of separate commissioners for America, England gave free rein to a set of men who in less than ten years dissolved the loyalty and mutual interest that had hitherto bound the empire together. Professor Dickerson has traced in detail the activities, of the American Customs Commissioners and of the officers who operated under their direction. What he finds is "customs racketeering," the use of technicalities in the law to trap American merchants and seize their ships (the officers received a third of the proceeds of ships condemned and sold for customs violations). Among those victimized were two leading figures of the Revolution, John Hancock of Boston and Henry Laurens of Charleston, South Carolina. Behind many of the famous incidents that provoked American hostility to England, including the Boston Massacre and the depredations of the Schooner *Gaspee,* Professor Dickerson sees the guiding hands of the Customs Commissioners.

The Navigation Acts and the American Revolution offers the most important new information about the Revolution produced in the past twenty-five years. The effect of it is to swing attention away from internal conflicts and back toward the question of home rule. It shows that the colonists had genuine grievances against England and may not have been influenced merely by propaganda or by a desire to evade taxes which they ought in equity to have paid. It does not, however, discuss directly the validity or consistency of colonial objections to Parliamentary taxations.

In *The Stamp Act Crisis: Prologue to Revolution* (1953), written in collaboration with Helen M. Morgan, I have examined the colonial arguments against the Sugar Act and the Stamp Act and found them more sweeping than has generally been supposed. When England first tried to tax Americans in 1764, they objected on principle to all taxation by Parliament and did not make the distinction between external and internal taxes so often attributed to them. They were not therefore guilty of all the inconsistencies they have been charged with. Their political ideas were not altogether static, but their attachment to principle was greater than twentieth-century historians have usually supposed. In a shorter book on the entire period from 1763 to 1789 (*The Birth of the Republic* [1956]) I have tried to describe the American search for principles of freedom and to see these years as a time of extraordinary unification rather than division. . . .

It would be wrong to leave the impression that the imperial, the social-economic, or the Namierist interpretation is now finished. Each has made a lasting contribution to our knowledge of the Revolutionary period. Each is still inspiring new studies. But the time has come, as I have suggested elsewhere ("The American Revolution: Revisions in Need of Revising," *William and Mary Quarterly,* third series, XIV [1957], 3–15) when we may begin to determine the limits of these interpretations. We should employ the new insights we have gained toward a better understanding of why men behaved as they did in 1776 or 1787, but we must not expand particular insights into a complete explanation. We must continue to ask, for we still do not fully know, what the Revolution was.

unit two

The Civil War

The American Civil War has had a unique impact upon the national consciousness. The fact that it was an internal struggle, a war between "brothers," gave it an intensity that has reverberated through the years. Wars against outsiders may be bitter, but family quarrels involve unusual depths of emotion. Americans have probably written and read more about the Civil War than any other conflict. Poets and novelists have vied with historians in dealing with Civil War themes, but historians have the responsibility to increase knowledge and understanding of this crucial struggle in American history.

Most early accounts of the Civil War were passionately partisan, though there were a few which denounced extremists on both sides. Southern writers tended to stress constitutional issues, or states' rights. Northern chroniclers gloried in the moral superiority of the Union cause. Historians of both the North and South emphasized economic and geographic distinctions between the sections. Many historians — both North and South — identified slavery as the cause of the conflict.

Although these early writings were influenced by the direct involvement of the authors, the seeds of most modern interpretations of the Civil War can be found in them. One of the most unusual features of Civil War historiography is the recurrence of older interpretations in modern accounts. Some present-day writers have revived the fiery partisanship of the 1840–1880 period. Those who stress moral objections to slavery as causes of war revert to the ideas of

Northern writers of the Civil War era. Modern writers and politicians, like the earlier historians, have also seen economic differences between the sections as the major irritant. Current historians who feel the war could and should have been avoided recall the views of peace advocates like Clement C. Vallandigham, leader in 1862 of the Peace Democrats, and Henry S. Foote, a member of the Confederate Congress who criticized Jefferson Davis for not accepting Lincoln's peace proposals.

As the Civil War recedes, there seems to be less agreement among historians as to its causes. Civil War history written since the turn of the century should be considered against the background of revolutionary changes since 1900. Industrialization and urbanization have altered the structure of American life. The United States experienced a severe depression and two great reform movements. Nations throughout the world felt the deep wounds of two world wars. America became a great world power, while totalitarian dictatorships rose to challenge democracy, and scientists, prompted by governments, developed weapons capable of destroying civilization.

Historians are rarely able to assume Olympian detachment from events in their own times. In their interpretive treatments of the Civil War, American historians of the twentieth century have inevitably been affected by these forces. The "confusion of voices" in the interpretation of the Civil War reflects the differing beliefs and attitudes of the present age. Important Civil War issues have not yet been laid to rest. This is somewhat dismaying to those who seek a "scientific history," one which progresses steadily toward a universally recognized truth.

The five Problems in this unit examine some of the modern interpretations. Problem 6 deals with the economic argument. Problem 7 stresses the cultural differences between the sections. In Problem 8 the source of the conflict is explained in terms of extremism and a failure of political leadership. Problem 9 presents a case for the central importance of moral considerations. In Problem 10 a contemporary historian summarizes various interpretations, concentrating on those written after 1940. He shows the extent to which one's conclusions depend on personal philosophical assumptions.

The Economic Interpretation
of the Civil War

During the Civil War and for a generation thereafter, historians explained the war by blaming one side or the other for it. As long as passions remained hot, partisans of the North or the South searched for those responsible for the great tragedy. Southerners blamed "Black Republican" aggressors, and Northerners the "Slave Power" conspiracy.

Northern writers pictured slavery as an evil institution and as the primary cause of the war. They saw the conflict as a struggle between good and evil, between freedom and servitude, and between democracy and aristocracy. In this struggle the North held a morally superior position. Southern historians insisted that the Northern attack upon the South was the main cause of the war. They said the South was fighting for freedom—freedom from a tyrannical central government that was destroying the rights of the states.

Taken as a whole, these conspiracy, or "devil," theories constituted the first general interpretation of the causes of the Civil War. Then as the years passed, sectional passions cooled. A second generation of historians emerged who wrote in an age of nationalism and sectional reconciliation. In the 1890's the absorbing interests of America were industrial growth, reform, and the Spanish-American War. Historians like James Ford Rhodes,

Edward Channing, and John Bach McMaster did not "blame" either side for the Civil War but found causes in impersonal factors.

Rhodes, the author of the seven-volume *History of the United States from the Compromise of 1850*, argued that the institution of slavery was the single cause of the war and "that if the negro had never been brought to America, our Civil War would not have occurred." Furthermore, he said, while slavery was a moral wrong, it had arisen because of the spread of cotton production, not because of evil Southerners. He also maintained that the North was right in the war, but the South was equally right in the Reconstruction period and that those who erred did so from good motives rather than from bad. Rhodes and other historians of the "nationalist" school aimed at fairness and objectivity. They found many Americans in their day receptive to this approach, for reconciliation between the sections was an immensely popular theme. These nationalist writers thus contributed a general restatement and a second major interpretation of the origins of the war.

Yet at the very time the nationalist viewpoint was receiving widespread approval, a new theory was developing. This new approach also reflected the revolutionary changes that were taking place in American life. In the half century after Appomattox, the simple, rural America of the past was rapidly becoming a complex industrial and urban society. This profound transformation created problems which led to the Populist and Progressive reform movements. The intellectual climate was changing; in literature, religion, education, law, and other fields new ideas were challenging older values.

Out of this climate there appeared a new group of historians who were deeply interested in contemporary social and economic problems, distribution of wealth, and the political power of economic groups. These historians were on the side of reform and progressivism. James Harvey Robinson, one of the founders of the new school, believed that history had value only when it was used as a tool to reform society. The most famous of this group was Charles Austin Beard, who grew up in the age of Populism and Progressivism and whose writing reflected the social ferment of the period. In the reading that follows Beard emphasizes the influence of economic factors in the origin of the Civil War. As the devil theories and the nationalist viewpoints were favorably received in their day, so Beard's interpretation was acclaimed in the 1920's. During the depression years of the 1930's, it virtually became the generally accepted view. As you read, consider the following questions:

1 Do you agree with Beard's thesis that slavery was not the fundamental issue in the period before the Civil War? Does he support his argument convincingly?

2   Could such economic issues as the tariff or homestead laws have precipitated the Civil War?

3   How does Beard dispense with the argument over states' rights as a cause of the Civil War? Do you agree with him?

4   Although Jefferson Davis and William H. Seward were on opposite sides of the struggle over slavery, can you find any similarity in their approach to the causes of the Civil War?

5   Had there been no Negro slavery in America, do you believe the Civil War would have occurred?

6   Seward's comparison of a political party to a joint stock company implies that politics is no more than a struggle between economic interest groups. Do you agree?

"THE SECOND AMERICAN REVOLUTION"

In 1913 when Charles Beard's famous book *An Economic Interpretation of the Constitution* was published, shocked conservatives accused him of desecrating the memory of the Founding Fathers by attributing selfish economic motives to them. For Beard, the key to understanding history was to be found in the struggles between economic interest groups. In *The Rise of American Civilization,* he used this "key" to analyze the causes of the Civil War. □ Reprinted with permission of The Macmillan Co., from *The Rise of American Civilization* by Charles A. Beard and Mary R. Beard. Volume 2, pp. 3–10, 36, 38–40, 51–54. Copyright © 1927 by The Macmillan Co., renewed 1955 by William Beard and Miriam B. Vagts.

Had the economic systems of the North and the South remained static or changed slowly without effecting immense dislocations in the social structure, the balance of power might have been maintained indefinitely by repeating the compensatory tactics of 1787, 1820, 1833, and 1850; keeping in this manner the inherent antagonisms within the bounds of diplomacy. But nothing was stable in the economy of the United States or in the moral sentiments associated with its diversities [in the 1860's].

Within each section of the country, the necessities of the productive system were generating portentous results. The periphery of the industrial vortex of the Northeast was daily enlarging, agriculture in the Northwest was being steadily supplemented by manufacturing, and the area of virgin soil open to exploitation by planters was diminishing with rhythmic regularity—shifting with mechanical precision the weights which statesmen had to adjust in their efforts to maintain the equilibrium of peace. Within each of the three sections also occurred an increasing intensity of social concentration as railways, the telegraph, and the press made travel and communication cheap and almost instantaneous, facilitating the centripetal process that was drawing people of similar economic status and parallel opinions into coöperative activities. . . .

As the years passed, the planting leaders of Jefferson's agricultural party [which had become known as the Democratic party by 1828] insisted with mounting fervor that the opposition, first of the Whigs and then of the Republicans, was at bottom an association of interests formed for the purpose of plundering productive management and labor on the land. And with steadfast insistence they declared that in the insatiable greed of their political foes lay the source of the dissensions which were tearing the country asunder. . . .

The fact that free-soil advocates waged war only on slavery in the territories was to Jefferson Davis [then United States Senator from Mississippi] conclusive proof of an underlying conspiracy against agriculture. He professed more respect for the abolitionist than for the free-soiler. The former, he said, is dominated by an honest conviction that slavery is wrong everywhere and that all men ought to be free; the latter does not assail slavery in the states—he merely wishes to abolish it in the territories that are in due course to be admitted to the Union.

With challenging directness, Davis turned upon his opponents in the Senate and charged them with using slavery as a blind to delude the unwary: "What do you propose, gentlemen of the Free-Soil party? Do you propose to better the condition of the slave? Not at all. What then do you propose? You say you are opposed to the expansion of slavery. . . . Is the slave to be benefited by it? Not at all. It is not humanity that influences you in the position which you now occupy before the country. . . . It is that you may have an opportunity of cheating us that you want to limit slave territory within circumscribed bounds. It is that you may have a majority in the Congress of the United States and convert the Government into an engine of northern aggrandizement. It is that your section may grow in power and prosperity upon treasures unjustly taken from the South, like the vampire bloated and gorged with the blood which it has secretly sucked from its victim . . . You desire to weaken the political power of the southern states; and why? Because you want, by an unjust system of legislation, to promote the industry of the New England states, at the expense of the people of the South and their industry."

Such in the mind of Jefferson Davis, fated to be president of the Confederacy, was the real purpose of the party which sought to prohibit slavery in the territories; that party did not declare slavery to be a moral disease calling for the severe remedy of the surgeon; it merely sought to keep bondage out of the new states as they came into the Union—with one fundamental aim in view, namely, to gain political ascendancy in the government of the United States and fasten upon the country an economic policy that meant the exploitation of the South for the benefit of northern capitalism.

But the planters were after all fighting against the census returns, as the phrase of the day ran current. The amazing growth of northern industries, the rapid extension of railways, the swift expansion of foreign trade to the ends of the earth, the attachment of the farming regions of the West to the centers of manufacture and finance through transportation and credit, the destruction of state consciousness by migration, the alien invasion, the erection of new commonwealths in the Valley of Democracy, the nationalistic drive of interstate commerce, the increase of population in the North, and the southward pressure of the capitalistic glacier all conspired to assure the ultimate triumph of what the orators were fond of calling "the free labor system." This was a dynamic thrust far too powerful for planters operating in a limited territory with incompetent labor on soil of diminishing fertility. Those who swept forward with it, exulting in the approaching triumph of machine industry, warned the planters of their ultimate subjection.

To statesmen of the invincible forces recorded in the census returns, the planting opposition was a huge, compact, and self-conscious economic association bent upon political objects—the possession of the government of the United States, the protection of its interests against adverse legislation, dominion over the territories, and enforcement of the national fugitive slave law [passed in 1850, it stipulated that an escaped slave could be seized in any free state and returned to his owner] throughout the length and breadth of the land. No phrase was more often on the lips of northern statesmen than "the slave power." The pages of the Congressional Globe bristled with references to "the slave system" and its influence over the government of the country. But it was left for [Senator] William H. Seward of New York to describe it with a fullness of familiar knowledge that made his characterization a classic.

Seward knew from experience that a political party was no mere platonic society engaged in discussing abstractions. "A party," he said, "is in one sense a joint stock association, in which those who contribute most direct the action and management of the concern. The slaveholders contributing in an overwhelming proportion to the capital strength of the Democratic party, they necessarily dictate and prescribe its policy. The inevitable caucus system enables them to do this with a show of fairness and justice." This class of slaveholders, consisting of only three hundred and forty-seven thousand persons, Seward went on to say, was spread from the banks of the Delaware to the banks of the Rio Grande; it possessed nearly all the real estate in that section, owned more than three million other "persons" who were denied all civil and political rights, and inhibited "freedom of speech, freedom of press, freedom of the ballot box, freedom of education, freedom of litera- ture, and freedom of popular assemblies. . . . The slaveholding class has become the governing power in each of the slaveholding states and it prac- tically chooses thirty of the sixty-two members of the Senate, ninety of the two hundred and thirty-three members of the House of Representatives, and one hundred and five of the two hundred and ninety-five electors of the President and Vice-President of the United States."

Becoming still more concrete, Seward accused the President [James Buchanan] of being "a confessed apologist of the slave-property class." Examining the composition of the Senate, he found the slave-owning group in possession of all the important committees. Peering into the House of Representatives he discovered no impregnable bulwark of freedom there. Nor did respect for judicial ermine compel him to spare the Supreme Court. With irony he exclaimed: "How fitting does the proclamation of its opening close with the invocation: 'God save the United States and this honorable court. . . .' The court consists of a chief justice and eight associate justices. Of these five were called from slave states and four from free states. The opinions and bias of each of them were carefully considered by the President and Senate when he was appointed. Not one of them was found wanting in soundness of politics, according to the slaveholder's exposition of the Con- stitution, and those who were called from the free states were even more distinguished in that respect than their brethren from the slaveholding states." . . .

Having described the gigantic operating structure of the slavocracy, Seward drew with equal power a picture of the opposing system found on "free labor." He surveyed the course of economy in the North—the growth of industry, the spread of railways, the swelling tide of European immigra- tion, and the westward roll of free farmers—rounding out the country, knit- ting it together, bringing "these antagonistic systems" continually into closer contact. Then he uttered those fateful words which startled conservative citizens from Maine to California—words of prophecy which proved to be brutally true—"the irrepressible conflict."

This inexorable clash, he said, was not "accidental, unnecessary, the work of interested or fanatical agitators and therefore ephemeral." No. "It is an irrepressible conflict between opposing and enduring forces." The hopes

of those who sought peace by appealing to slave owners to reform themselves were as chaff in a storm. "How long and with what success have you
waited already for that reformation? Did any property class ever so reform
itself? Did the patricians in old Rome, the noblesse or clergy in France?
The landholders in Ireland? The landed aristocracy in England? Does the
slaveholding class even seek to beguile you with such a hope? Has it not
become rapacious, arrogant, defiant?" All attempts at compromise were "vain
and ephemeral." There was accordingly but one supreme task before the
people of the United States—the task of confounding and overthrowing "by
one decisive blow the betrayers of the Constitution and freedom forever."
In uttering this indictment, this prophecy soon to be fulfilled with such
appalling accuracy, Seward stepped beyond the bounds of cautious politics
and read himself out of the little group of men who were eligible for the
Republican nomination in 1860. Frantic efforts to soften his words by
explanations and additions could not appease his critics.

Given an irrepressible conflict which could be symbolized in such unmistakable patterns by competent interpreters of opposing factions, a transfer
of the issues from the forum to the field, from the conciliation of diplomacy
to the decision of arms was bound to come. . . .

. . . [It] must be apparent that the forces which produced the irrepressible conflict were very complex in nature and yet the momentous struggle
has been so often reduced by historians to simple terms that a reëxamination
of the traditional thesis has become one of the tasks of the modern age. On
the part of northern writers it was long the fashion to declare that slavery
was the cause of the conflict between the states. Such for example was the
position taken by James Ford Rhodes and made the starting point of his
monumental work. . . .

With reference to the popular northern view of the conflict, there stands
the stubborn fact that at no time during the long gathering of the storm
did [William Lloyd] Garrison's abolition creed rise to the dignity of a first
rate political issue in the North. Nobody but agitators, beneath the contempt of the towering statesmen of the age, ever dared to advocate it. No
great political organization even gave it the most casual indorsement.

When the abolitionists launched the Liberty party in the campaign of
1844 to work for emancipation, . . . the voters answered their plea for "the
restoration of equality of political rights among men" in a manner that
demonstrated the invincible opposition of the American people. Out of more
than two and a half million ballots cast in the election, only sixty-five
thousand were recorded in favor of the Liberty candidate. That was America's answer to the call for abolition; and the advocates of that policy never

again ventured to appeal to the electorate by presenting candidates on such a radical platform. . . .

Even the Republican party, in the campaign of 1856 coming hard on the act of defiance [Kansas-Nebraska Act] which swept away the Missouri compact, won little more than one-third the active voters to the cause of restricting the slavery area. When transformed after four more years into a homestead and high tariff party pledged merely to liberty in the territories, the Republicans polled a million votes fewer than the number cast for the opposing factions and rode into power on account of the divided ranks of the enemy. Such was the nation's reply to the anti-slavery agitation from the beginning of the disturbance until the cannon shot at Fort Sumter opened a revolution. . . .

Since, therefore, the abolition of slavery never appeared in the platform of any great political party, since the only appeal ever made to the electorate on that issue was scornfully repulsed, since the spokesman of the Republicans emphatically declared that his party never intended to interfere with slavery in the states in any shape or form, it seems reasonable to assume that the institution of slavery was not the fundamental issue during the epoch preceding the bombardment of Fort Sumter.

Nor can it be truthfully said, as southern writers were fond of having it, that a tender and consistent regard for the rights of states and for a strict construction of the Constitution was the prime element in the dispute that long divided the country. As a matter of record, from the foundation of the republic, all factions were for high nationalism or low provincialism upon occasion according to their desires at the moment, according to turns in the balance of power. New England nullified federal law when her commerce was affected by the War of 1812 and came out stanchly for liberty and union, one and inseparable, now and forever, in 1833 when South Carolina attempted to nullify a tariff act. Not long afterward, the legislature of Massachusetts, dreading the overweening strength of the Southwest, protested warmly against the annexation of Texas and resolved that "such an act of admission would have no binding force whatever on the people of Massachusetts." . . .

When the modern student examines all the verbal disputes over the nature of the Union—the arguments employed by the parties which operated and opposed the federal government between the adoption of the Constitution and the opening of the Civil War—he can hardly do otherwise than conclude that the linguistic devices used first on one side and then on the other were not derived from inherently necessary concepts concerning the intimate essence of the federal system. The roots of the controversy lay elsewhere—in social groupings founded on differences in climate, soil, industries, and labor systems, in divergent social forces, rather than varying degrees of righteousness and wisdom or what . . . [has been called] "the magnetism of great personalities." . . .

In the spring of 1861 the full force of the irrepressible conflict burst upon the hesitant and bewildered nation and for four long years the clash of arms filled the land with its brazen clangor. For four long years the anguish, the calamities, and the shocks of the struggle absorbed the energies of the multitudes, blared in the headlines of the newspapers, and loomed . . . in the minds of the men and women who lived . . . in that age. . . .

. . . For years the agony of it hung like a pall over the land. And yet with strange swiftness the cloud was lifted and blown away. Merciful grass spread its green mantle over the cruel scars and the gleaming red splotches sank into the hospitable earth.

It was then that the economist and lawyer, looking more calmly on the scene, discovered that the armed conflict had been only one phase of the cataclysm, a transitory phase; that at bottom the so-called Civil War, or the War between the States, in the light of Roman analogy, was a social war, ending in the unquestioned establishment of a new power in the government, making vast changes in the arrangement of classes, in the accumulation and distribution of wealth, in the course of industrial development, and in the Constitution inherited from the Fathers. Merely by the accidents of climate, soil, and geography was it a sectional struggle. If the planting interest had been scattered evenly throughout the industrial region, had there been a horizontal rather than a perpendicular cleavage, the irrepressible conflict would have been resolved by other methods and accompanied by other logical defense mechanisms.

In any event neither accident nor rhetoric should be allowed to obscure the intrinsic character of that struggle. If the operations by which the middle classes of England broke the power of the king and the aristocracy are to be known collectively as the Puritan Revolution, if the series of acts by which the bourgeois and peasants of France overthrew the king, nobility, and clergy is to be called the French Revolution, then accuracy compels us to characterize by the same term the social cataclysm in which the capitalists, laborers, and farmers of the North and West drove from power in the national government the planting aristocracy of the South. Viewed under the light of universal history, the fighting was a fleeting incident; the social revolution was the essential, portentous outcome.

To be sure the battles and campaigns of the epoch are significant to the military strategist; the tragedy and heroism of the contest furnish inspiration to patriots and romance to the makers of epics. But the core of the vortex lay elsewhere. It was in the flowing substance of things limned by statistical reports on finance, commerce, capital, industry, railways, and agriculture, by provisions of constitutional law, and by the pages of statute books— prosaic muniments which show that the so-called civil war was in reality a Second American Revolution and in a strict sense, the First.

The physical combat that punctuated the conflict merely hastened the inevitable. As was remarked at the time, the South was fighting against the census returns—census returns that told of accumulating industrial capital, multiplying captains of industry, expanding railway systems, widening acres tilled by free farmers. Once the planting and the commercial states, as the Fathers with faithful accuracy described them, had been evenly balanced; by 1860 the balance was gone.

PROBLEM 7

The Conflict of Cultures

One of the most persistent theories about the coming of the Civil War has been the "conflict of cultures" interpretation. Writers who lived in the Civil War period often spoke of the war as a struggle between two different and antagonistic societies. American historians of the twentieth century developed a strong interest in cultural history, and schools and colleges placed greater emphasis upon courses in civilizations and cultures. "Cultural history" rests on the premise that one must study the "whole" society—its politics, economics, art, religion, philosophy, and social customs—in order to understand that society.

Partly influenced by this view, some historians have explained the Civil War in a broader context than such single considerations as states' rights, or economic determinism, or slavery. In this process some have emphasized race, some the different social systems, others nationalism, but all have renounced Beard's economic interpretation as too narrow and confining. In *Ordeal of the Union,* a major synthesis of the Civil War, Allan Nevins sharply rejected the economic view. He said, "Of all the monistic explanations for the drift to war, that posited upon supposed economic causes is the flimsiest."

Modern American historians recognized that nationalistic fervor contributed to the coming of two world wars. They studied the relationship of nationalism and group behavior to historical events. When they turned to the Civil War, some of them saw that the struggle was essentially a conflict of cultures and that Southern nationalism was a strong and pervasive force of crucial importance.

What was it that made the South of the nineteenth century different from the rest of the country? Obvious distinctions were climate, population, the plantation system, cotton, and slavery. One influential Southern historian, Ulrich B. Phillips, called "race" the central theme of Southern history.

It is easy to exaggerate the actual differences between North and South and to assume that they were two absolutely distinct and separate sections. Many parts of the North, however, were just as rural as the South, and both sections had a common history and heritage.

Within the South itself there existed varieties and differences—mountain, seaboard, and upland districts, the black belt, and the Southwest, each distinct in some ways from the others. Yet there was still one South. Wilbur Cash, author of *The Mind of the South,* said that if the South was not quite a nation within a nation, it was the nearest thing to it. Historians emphasizing the "conflict of cultures" interpretation agree with this argument. They would describe as most accurate the explanation by Senator James M. Mason of Virginia on the eve of the Civil War: "I look upon it, then, Sir, as a war of sentiment and opinion by one form of society against another form of society."

Two readings are included in Problem 7. In the first Allan Nevins describes economic and social conditions which worked toward the formation of two contrasting societies, while, in the second reading, Rollin G. Osterweis discusses romantic nationalism in the Old South.

As you read, consider the following questions:

1 Would Nevins agree that cultural differences between the North and the South were primarily caused by slavery?

2 How much importance do you attach to Nevins' emphasis on the absence of a strong middle-class agricultural community in the South? Would a "really strong Southern yeomanry" have prevented the Civil War?

3 What is the essential difference between Beard's interpretation and the explanations of Nevins and Osterweis? Are the economic and cultural conflict interpretations related to each other? Is Nevins or Osterweis closest to Beard?

4 Do you agree with Osterweis that the South did not wish to alter the existing political organization? How can this be proven?

5 Osterweis claims that the talk about states' rights was merely "window dressing" for Southern rights. Do you agree?

6 Did Southern nationalism differ in character from the American nationalism of the Revolutionary War era? Was there a distinctive Northern nationalism prior to the Civil War?

I

SOUTHERN NATIONALISM

In *Ordeal of the Union* and in *The Emergence of Lincoln,* Allan Nevins made the first attempt since the days of James Ford Rhodes to write a comprehensive history of the background of the Civil War. In the excerpt that follows, he presents an insight into Southern culture. □ Selection from *Ordeal of the Union,* Volume 2, pp. 540–544, 553, 554, by Allan Nevins (copyright © 1947 Charles Scribner's Sons) is issued by permission of Charles Scribner's Sons.

Asked just where, in detail, the differences of the South lay, we can answer under numerous headings.

The white population of the South was far more largely Anglo-Saxon than that of the North, for despite its numerous Germans, its hundred thousand Irish folk by 1860, its French Huguenots, and others, it was one of the purest British stocks in the world. Its dominant attitudes, particularly as to the color line, were Anglo-Saxon. Its life was not merely rural, but rural after a special pattern; for the section was dotted over with large holdings representing great capital values and employing large bodies of slaves. It was a land of simple dogmatism in religion; of Protestant solidarity, of people who believed every word of the Bible, and of faith frequently refreshed by emotional revivalism. Its churches provided an emphasis on broadly social values contrasting with the intellectualization of morals to be found in the North. In the South the yoke of law and government rested more lightly upon the individual than in other sections. Counties, often sprawling in extent, were the chief units of local administration; the States followed the rule that the best government was the least government; and the nation was held at arm's length.

The South drew from its economic position a special set of tenets, naturally accepting Francis Wayland's [an American educator] condemnation of [tariff] protection as a violation of morality and common sense. With equal inevitability, it drew from its minority position in the political fabric another special set of doctrines. It was a country in which romantic and hedonistic impulses, born of the opulence of nature, had freer rein than in the North. The phrases "the merry South," "the sunny South," connoted a great deal. . . . The remote quality attaching to much Southern life, which made some travellers feel they had dropped into another world, and the sharp contrast of races, added to the atmosphere of romance.

To a far greater degree than the North, the South was a land of class stratification and vestigial feudalism. Various explanations were given for this fact. One was later repeated by N. S. Shaler [an American educator] when he remarked that Southerners were descendants of that portion of the English who were least modernized, and who "still retained a large element of the feudal notion." It is now known that no such distinction existed between Northern and Southern colonists, for honest middle-class folk, not feudal-minded cavaliers, made up the bulk of Virginia as of Massachusetts settlers. Slavery, the large plantation, and the agrarian cast of life, with some traditional inheritances from colonial days, accounted for the class structure. "Slavery helped feudalism," correctly remarked a Southern writer, "and feudalism helped slavery, and the Southern people were largely the outcome of the interaction of these two formative principles."

The great colonial plantations, established along the South Atlantic seaboard and in Louisiana in days when tobacco, rice, and sugar reigned without thought of a new monarch named cotton, had possessed much the atmosphere and influence of the English manors. Even North Carolina had its first families, the Winstons, Taylors, and Byrds of the Tidewater. The planters enjoyed the social dignities and political leadership of the English squires. They revered the old order, dispensed hospitality, and benignly guided their inferiors in Sir Roger de Coverley style [the ideal of the early eighteenth-century squire]. As a rigorous code of personal honor was enforced by the duel rather than by law, and gentlefolk deemed themselves highly sensitive to slights, they developed a punctilious courtesy. Yet the ideal Southern gentleman seldom appeared in perfection; politeness, gallantry, and dignity had often to be reconciled with the sudden passion of a Preston Brooks [Southern Congressman who assaulted Senator Charles Sumner in the Senate], and, as [writer] James Branch Cabell has mentioned, a weakness for miscegenation. A planter who entertained much, thought much of the good old times, and handed down his home acres to his oldest son even when primogeniture was no more, naturally made much of family ties. Kinship was counted to remote cousinhood, the penniless spinster who bore the family name had a welcome place in the household, and summer visitings . . . were common. Family did much to knit the South together.

Yet class lines can easily be overemphasized, for they were subject to powerful solvents. The fact that many a poor farmer and rich planter looked back to a common ancestor was one; wealth in such instances usually bowed before relationship. The fact that all white men had a sense of solidarity as against the Negro, and as against the encroaching North, also tended to reduce class stratification. . . . As in the North the advancing frontier was an unquestionable force for democracy, in the South it at least modified the features of aristocracy. . . .

But taken as a section, stretching from the Atlantic to the Father of Waters and from the Ohio to the Gulf, the South had a life of far more aristocratic tone than the North. Both the central weakness of the South, and the main flaw in American social homogeneity, lay in the want of a great predominant body of intelligent, independent, thoughtful, and educated farmers in the slave States to match the similar body at the North. The nation had always drawn most of its sturdy common sense and integrity of character from its farmers. A really strong Southern yeomanry could have clasped hands with Northern tillers of the soil. But the plantation system was inimical to any such body. Whether developing or declining, it wasted soil and toil, reduced the mass of blacks and whites to poverty, kept them in ignorance, and destroyed their hopes. It was not a preparation for the appearance of an independent, industrious farmer class, but a "preface to peasantry." It gave the South the "forgotten man" that [an American journalist] Walter Hines Page described in his memorable address at Greensboro [North Carolina] a generation later; men too poor, ignorant, and politician-beguiled to be discontented with their poverty, ignorance, and docility.

With all its natural gaiety, simplicity, and love of olden ways the South combined a trait common in countries with unhappy institutions, like Spain, and in lands left behind by modern progress, like Ireland; the trait of uneasy defensiveness. At the beginning of the century most Southerners had believed that Virginia would keep her primacy among the States in wealth, population, and influence, that their whole section would grow faster than the chilly North, and that their grasp on the national tiller would be unshaken. That belief had withered before the Mexican War. Clear-eyed men realized that in nearly all material elements of civilization the North had far outstripped them; and they knew that slavery stood indicted not merely as a moral wrong, but as responsible for this painful lag in progress. In the Southern mind a defensive mechanism clicked into operation. Slavery? It was a blessing. The Negro? They best understood him. "Whatever defects may belong to our system, it certainly has the merit of preserving the Negro and improving his situation. Look at the moderating influences. Look [at] their own advance in health, comfort, virtue, and numbers." Progress? No sane man wanted the "calculating avarice" that, as Calhoun said, marked the factory owner driving his wage slaves.

Hand in hand with this defensive attitude, as all observers noted, went a passionate Southern pride. . . . An aristocratic society is always proud, and we might trace far back into colonial times the Southern conviction of superiority to Northern and British shilling-grabbers. Many slaveholders liked to talk, at first confidentially but later in speeches frankly addressed to Northern ears, of the defects of shirtsleeves democracy, Yankee industrialism, and the vomit of European slums. More and more, this pride was related to that inferiority complex which is so often a mark of superior peoples set amid unfavorable environments. The pride of the ruling class was bulwarked by an intellectual factor, the influence of the old writers—Hobbes in government, Dryden in poetry, [Edward Hyde, Earl of] Clarendon in history—who regarded aristocracy as the best form of social control.

In none of its varied manifestations was sectional pride more dangerous than in its constant assertions of superior fighting power. "If it comes to blows between the North and the South," a Yankee heard William Gilmore Simms [an American writer] exclaim, "we shall crush you as I would crush an egg." John B. Gordon [an officer in the Confederate army] heard a judge remark that in the event of war, the South could "whip the Yankees with children's pop-guns." The well-born Southerner was convinced that he was a man of far more spirit and resource than the Northern counterjumper [a salesman in a shop]. Nothing struck William H. Russell [a British war correspondent] more forcibly, in his travels over the South just before the Civil War, than the widespread conviction that the free States would never fight, or if they did would be quickly put in their places. A later writer on "the fighting South" has ascribed its militancy to the old habit of living dangerously, and to a depth of conviction, a 'totality of pure-hearted affirmation' natural in a simple society. Perhaps more important were the conditions of Southern life, with much hunting, general use of horses, and frequent marksmanship contests; the existence of two fine schools of war, the Virginia Military Institute at Lexington, and the South Carolina Military Academy or "Citadel" at Charleston; and the memory of Southern prowess in the Mexican War. The leading officers, Scott, Taylor, Quitman, Twiggs, and Davis, were all Southrons—if one forgot Kearny or Worth. Indeed, in what war had not Southern commanders stood foremost? . . .

Altogether, South and North by 1857 were rapidly becoming separate peoples. The major Protestant denominations had broken in twain; one major party, the Whigs, had first split in half and then disappeared; press, pulpit, and education all showed a deepening cleavage. . . .

The Southerners loved the Union, for their forefathers had helped build it, and the gravestones of their patriot soldiers strewed the land. But they wanted a Union in which they could preserve their peculiar institutions, ancient customs, and well-loved ways of life and thought. They knew that all the main forces of modern society were pressing to create a more closely unified nation, and to make institutions homogeneous even if not absolutely uniform. Against this they recoiled; they wanted a hegemony, a loose confederacy, not a unified nation and a standardized civilization. They regarded the Union as an association of sovereign States and an alliance of regions that possessed national attributes. The North wishes to dictate to us on the slavery question, wrote Simms in 1852. "But we are a people, *a nation,* with arms in our hands, and in sufficient numbers to compel the respect of *other nations;* and we shall never submit the case to the judgment of *another people,* until they show themselves of superior virtue and intellect."

This schism in culture struck into the very substance of national life. Differences of thought, taste, and ideals gravely accentuated the misunderstandings caused by the basic economic and social differences; the differences between a free labor system and a slave labor system, between a semi-industrialized economy of high productiveness and an agrarian economy of low productiveness. An atmosphere was created in which emotions grew feverish; in which every episode became a crisis, every jar a shock.

II

"A NATION AMONG NATIONS"

Believing that society in the Old South rested on a tripod—cotton, Negro slavery, and romantic nationalism, Rollin G. Osterweis concentrates on romantic nationalism, the neglected leg of the tripod, in the following excerpt. ☐ Rollin G. Osterweis, *Romanticism and Nationalism in the Old South,* pp. 132–138, 150, 152–154. New Haven: Yale University Press. Copyright © 1949.

The idea of Southern nationalism, which developed chiefly in South Carolina during the decade before the Civil War, was the most ambitious romantic manifestation of the antebellum period. It is not unnatural that this energy-demanding and forward-looking trend should have been cradled in a hard-headed community. These were people anxious to lead—possessing political and intellectual talent, accumulated wealth, influential periodicals, and a past history of fiery, independent thinking. Around 1850 the Cotton Kingdom was looking for leadership; and the Palmetto State stood ready to fill that need. It was soon ahead of the times, waiting for the rest of the South to catch up with its daring plans. . . .

The idea of Southern nationalism emerged about 1850 out of an experience mainly native and nonromantic. During the ten years before the war, it took on a distinctive, romantic coloration. . . . By . . . [1850], certainly, a group consciousness had developed, an *ethnocentrism,* an impulse for Southern nationalism. The impulse was so similar to the ideas of romantic nationalism, then prevalent in Europe, that it offered a natural affinity for those ideas. . . .

The Carolinian conviction that Southerners comprised a separate cultural unit grew stronger from the concomitant belief that the rest of the country possessed an inferior civilization. So obvious was this attitude by 1860 that the correspondent of the London *Times* could grasp it completely. In a letter dated "Charleston, April 30, 1861," William Howard Russell declared:

"Believe a Southern man as he believes himself and you must regard New England and the kindred states as the birthplace of impurity of mind among men and of unchastity in women—the home of Free Love, of Fourierism, of Infidelity, of Abolitionism, of false teachings in political economy and in social life; a land saturated with the drippings of rotten philosophy, with the poisonous infections of a fanatic press; without honor or modesty; whose wisdom is paltry cunning, whose valor and manhood have been swallowed up in a corrupt, howling demagogy, and in the marts of dishonest commerce. . . ."

The men of the romantic age rarely used the word "nationalist" to describe themselves; and if it is used about them, care must be taken to place the modifier "cultural" in front of it. The nationalism of the romantic thinkers was a cultural nationalism, with the emphasis on "peoples," who were the architects and transmitters of distinct cultures. To these thinkers, "the idea of imposing any nation's ways, speech, or art upon another was repellent." . . . Herder, Wordsworth, Victor Hugo, speaking in the names of German, English, and French romanticisms, all exemplify belief in a non-aggressive, cultural nationalism.

The romantic view did imply longing, striving, and, if necessary, struggling to give expression to repressed cultural nationalism. . . .

"Nationalism," according to Hans Kohn, "is first and foremost a state of mind, an act of consciousness, which since the French Revolution has become more and more common to mankind." . . . But the concept, in its developed stage, goes beyond the idea of the group animated by common consciousness. It comprehends also the striving by the group to find expression in the organized activity of a sovereign state. Thus, the nationalism of the nineteenth century was a fusion of an attitude of mind with a particular political form. . . .

Southern nationalism . . . stressed the peculiarities of its particular traditions and institutions. In common with the romantic nationalisms of central Europe in the nineteenth century, the frontiers of the existing state and the rising nationality did not coincide. The movement expanded in protest against, and in conflict with, the de facto government. The objective was not to alter the existing political organization, as in the case of the thirteen colonies, but to redraw boundaries that would conform to mythical but credited ethnographic needs. That the realities behind the myth were the institution of Negro slavery and the plantation system do not affect the situation. They merely provide the identifying features.

The evolution of the idea of Southern nationalism, by 1860, was thus in the general stream of mid-nineteenth-century romantic thinking. "The Age of Nationalism," Professor Kohn suggests, "stressed national pasts and traditions against the rationalism of the eighteenth century with its emphasis on the common sense of civilization." The tendency in Europe was to weave the myths of the past and the dreams of the future into the picture of an ideal fatherland—an ideal to be striven for with deep emotional fervor.

This tendency was adapted to the Southern scene. From the past Virginia resurrected her George Washington, who had led an earlier crusade for independence; Maryland recalled her heroes in [James Ryder] Randall's stirring stanzas; Carolina cherished the cult of Calhoun; Louisiana pointed to her proud Creole heritage.

All this hewed to the line of romantic nationalism in Europe, where "each new nation looked for its justification to its national heritage—often reinterpreted to suit the supposed needs of the situation—and strove for its glorification." . . .

As soon as it was clear that the United States had elected a president commited to an anti-slavery platform, the South Carolina legislature voted to call a State convention. The delegates met at Columbia on December 17, 1860, fully conscious that they were about to sign an ordinance of secession. Because of a case of small pox in the town, they adjourned to Charleston on the eighteenth. Two days later, they voted unanimously to take their State out of the Union. The proceedings of the convention are significant, for they indicate that the delegates were thinking in far bigger terms than the secession of South Carolina. . . .

The *Journal* of the convention makes it perfectly clear that the men present were confident that they were launching a movement for a Southern confederacy. When the first meeting took place, commissioners from Alabama and Mississippi, appointed by their respective governors, joined the group. Letters of encouragement arrived from the states of Florida and Arkansas. Georgia offered volunteers in case South Carolina's action should lead to armed reprisals. . . .

The chips were down at the South Carolina secession convention. People recognized that most of the former talk about State rights had been window dressing. It was Southern rights that they were thinking about. . . .

That most astute of all Southern historians, Ulrich Phillips, maintained that State rights formed no object of devotion among the antebellum leaders for their own sake but only as a means of securing Southern rights. "State sovereignty," he pithily explained, "was used to give the insignia of legality to a stroke for national independence."

Regarding the fact that the framers of the Confederate Constitution gave official sanction to the State rights principle, Phillips concluded that this was, in large part, a mere saving of face. He said, "The movement was not so much a flying from the old center as a flying to the new; and it was not by chance that Timrod wrote in 1861, 'at last we are a nation among nations,' and entitled his poem of celebration 'Ethnogenesis.' "

Phillips' allusion to the poem "Ethnogenesis" is a happy one. He felt that "it was not by chance" that Timrod wrote in the vein that he did, with the emphasis on Southern nationalism. Nor was it by chance, either—it should be added—that he who wrote in this vein and who called his poem "Ethnogenesis" was a South Carolina romantic poet. In Henry Timrod's State, and among Henry Timrod's friends, the idea of Southern nationalism had matured. Who better could hail the meeting of the first Southern Congress, at Montgomery, with these lines?

> Hath not the morning dawned with added light?
> And shall not evening call another star
> Out of the infinite regions of the night,
> To mark this day in heaven? At last we are
> A nation among nations; and the world
> Shall soon behold in many a distant port
> Another flag unfurled!

PROBLEM 8

The Needless War

The belief that the Civil War was inevitable is one of the common themes in the interpretations examined so far in this volume. This view was symbolized in the title of Arthur C. Cole's book *The Irrepressible Conflict, 1850–1865*. Many historians, at least in the Northern part of the country, believed that the results of the Civil War were generally good because the Union was preserved and slavery was ended.

Yet the duration of any dominant view regarding the causes of the Civil War has been relatively short. Even in the 1920's and 1930's, when the Beard thesis was widely accepted, a new "revisionist" interpretation was already emerging.

It flowered in the 1940's and 1950's, notably in the works of Avery Craven and James G. Randall. Writing in an era of postwar tension, the revisionist historians boldly asserted that the Civil War had been neither good nor inevitable but rather a tragic and frightful mistake.

James G. Randall was a Lincoln scholar and an authority on the Civil War period. He argued that most Americans, in the North and in the South, did not want the war to come. When Northerners voted for Lincoln in 1860, they did not vote for war, nor did the Southerners when they voted for

John Breckenridge. They dreaded its coming, as Mr. Lincoln said in his Second Inaugural Address. Why, then, did it come? Because, said the revisionist historian, the extremists and agitators on both sides so inflamed opinion and emotions that they finally dragged the entire nation into a bloody and senseless catastrophe.

Randall, Craven, and other revisionists have been high in their praise of the various peace proposals that were made in 1860 and 1861. In revisionist writings Stephen Douglas emerged as a man of greater stature than attributed to him by earlier writers. Douglas was a middle-of-the-roader who was for peace and for a continuation of the Union half-free and half-slave. Randall considered this attitude the only sound position, for, he believed, slavery would have died out eventually simply because it could not have survived in an industrial society.

Because the revisionist interpretation is partly psychological—with its emphasis upon emotions, extremist mentality, and mass psychology—it raises serious questions for the historian. Is human behavior predictable? How can anyone ever know whether some great historical event was bound to happen? Does man have sufficient rationality to avoid war?

The strongest appeal of the thesis that the Civil War was unnecessary may be to the emotions of modern war-weary society, which possesses the weapons of ultimate destruction. To reject completely revisionist interpretation is to reject the idea that man can control his world.

Many Americans have not been willing to make that rejection, and in the middle years of the twentieth century, the "blundering generation" interpretation captured the support of a large and influential group of American historians.

As you read the selection by Randall in Problem 8, consider the following questions:

1   In debunking the romance of the Civil War, does Randall contribute to greater understanding of its causes?

2   Do you feel that Randall is convincing in his attack on the economic and cultural interpretations of the Civil War?

3   Would Randall's evaluation of Civil War causation be equally pertinent to analysis of the American Revolution?

4   If the Civil War was brought on by fanatics, what created the fanatics?

5   Note Randall's statement: "As to wars, the ones that have not happened are perhaps best to study." What seems to be his motivation in writing this essay? Do you think he properly fulfills the function of the historian?

EXTREMISM, FANATICISM, AND BOGUS LEADERSHIP

Scorning romantic notions about the Civil War and bitterly opposing all war, James G. Randall believed there was something psychopathic and irrational in the origins of armed conflicts. □ J. G. Randall, "The Blundering Generation." Lincoln, Nebraska: *The Mississippi Valley Historical Review*, Volume 27, Number 1, June 1940, pp. 3-4, 6-11, 13-16. Copyright © 1940 by the Mississippi Valley Historical Association.

When one visits a moving picture, or reads [Joseph] Hergesheimer's *Swords and Roses*, which is much the same thing, he may gather the impression that the Civil War, fought in the days before mechanized divisions, aerial bombs, and tanks, was a kind of *chanson de geste* [song of heroic deeds] in real life. "The Civil War in America," writes Hergesheimer, "was the last of all wars fought in the grand manner. It was the last romantic war, when army corps fought as individuals and lines of assault . . . charged the visible enemy." "The war created a heroism . . . that clad fact in the splendor of battle flags." Hergesheimer feeds his readers chunks of sombre beauty, winterless climate, air stirred with faint cool music, fine houses, Spanish moss and cypress, trumpet vine and bay blossom, live oaks and linden, bridal wreath, japonica, moonflower, and honeysuckle. In his foreword to "Dear Blanche" he writes: "Here is a book of swords . . . of old-fashioned dark roses. . . . [of] the simpler loveliness of the past." His pages live up to the foreword. . . . Of "Jeb" Stuart [General J. E. B. Stuart, Confederate cavalry leader] he says: "Ladies in Maryland gave him the spurs and ladies wherever he chanced to be gave him the rosebuds. . . . Naturally he was in the cavalry. He was different. . . . [He] wore a brown felt hat . . . with . . . sweeping black plume; . . . his boots in action were heavy, . . . afterwards he changed them for immaculate boots of patent leather worked with gold thread; but he danced as well as fought in his spurs."

The picture is filled in with red-lined cape, French sabre, yellow sash and tassels, The Bugles Sang Truce, The Dew is on the Blossom, orders given when asleep, animal vitality dancing in brilliant eyes.

Escapists may put what they will between the covers of a book; unfortunately the historian must be a realist. Whatever may be the thrill, or the emotional spree, of treating the Civil War romantically, it may be assumed that this has not been neglected. This paper, therefore, will attempt a very different task, that of weighing some Civil War realities, examining some of the irrational ideas of war "causation," and pondering some aspects of the Civil War mind. . . .

"Jeb" Stuart may have worn gold spurs, but the common soldier was more familiar with fleas. Sashes may have adorned generals but privates were often in rags. It was reported that one of the army surgeons boarded for an entire winter on Sanitary Commission stores. Camps were dirty, sanitation was faulty, cooking was shiftless. Reporting on one of the hospitals, an inspector referred to a leaky roof, broken glass, dirty stairs, insufficient sanitary facilities, and unclean disgusting beds. The soldier who was brutally struck by a sentry of his own company or who contracted malaria would hardly think of his experience as a thing of romance. Without exposing all the euphemisms that obscure the truth of this subject, it may be noted that the great majority of Union deaths were from causes medically regarded as preventable, leaving aside the cynical assumption that war itself is not preventable. Pneumonia, typhus, cholera, miasmic fever, and the like hardly find their way into the pages of war romance, but they wrought more havoc than bayonets and guns. Where there was danger of infection the rule-of-thumb principle of the Civil War surgeon was to amputate, and from operating tables, such as they were, at Gettysburg, arms and legs were carried away in wagon loads. Marching was hatefully wearisome, desertion was rampant, corruption was rife. Individual injustices of the war were shocking. Some generals got credit that was undeserved, others were broken by false report or slandered by an investigating committee of Congress. The men who languished in prison were several times more numerous than those stopped by bullets.

That there was heroism in the war is not doubted, but to thousands the war was as romantic as prison rats and as gallant as typhoid or syphilis.

One does not often speak or read of the war in reality, of its blood and filth, of mutilated flesh, and other revolting things. This restraint is necessary, but it ought to be recognized that the war is not presented when one writes of debates in Congress, of flanking movements, of retreats and advances, of cavalry and infantry, of divisions doing this and brigades doing that. In the sense of full realism war cannot be discussed. The human mind will not stand for it. For the very word "war" the realist would have to substitute some such term as "organized murder" or "human slaughterhouse." In drama as distinguished from melodrama murder often occurs offstage. In most historical accounts, especially military narratives, the war is offstage in that its stench and hideousness do not appear.

With all the recent revisionist studies it is difficult to achieve a full realization of how Lincoln's generation stumbled into a ghastly war, how it blundered during four years of indecisive slaughter, and how the triumph of the Union was spoiled by the manner in which the victory was used. In the hateful results of the war over long decades one finds partisanship at its worst. To see the period as it was is to witness uninspired spectacles of prejudice, error, intolerance, and selfish grasping. The Union army was inefficiently raised, poorly administered, and often badly commanded. In government there was a deadlock, cross purpose, and extravagance. One can say that Lincoln was honest, but not that the country was free from corruption during the Lincoln administration. There was cotton plundering, army-contract graft, and speculative greed. Where Lincoln was at his best, where he was moderate, temperate, and far-seeing, he did not carry his party with him. Even those matters dissociated from the war, such as homesteading and railroad extension, came to be marred by exploitation and crooked finance. The period of the Civil War and the era of Jim Fisk and Jay Gould were one and the same generation.

If it was a "needless war," a "repressible conflict," as scholars now believe, then indeed was the generation misled in its unctuous fury. To suppose that the Union could not have been continued or slavery outmoded without the war and without the corrupt concomitants of the war, is hardly an enlightened assumption. If one questions the term "blundering generation," let him inquire how many measures of the time he would wish copied or repeated if the period were to be approached with a clean slate and to be lived again. Most of the measures are held up as things to be avoided.

Of course it is not suggested that the generation of the sixties had any copyright on blundering. It is not that democracy was at fault. After all, civil war has not become chronic on these shores, as it has in some nations where politics of force is the rule. One can at least say that the Civil War was exceptional; that may be the best thing that can be said about it. A fuller measure of democracy would probably have prevented the war or at least have mitigated its abuses. To overlook many decades of American democracy and take the Civil War period as its test, would be to give an unfair appraisal.

Nor does this probing of blunders involve lack of respect for the human beings of that generation. As individuals we love and admire them, these men and women who look at us from the tintypes and Brady photographs of the sixties, though we may have "malice toward some." The distortions and errors of the time were rather a matter of mass thinking, of social solidification, and of politics.

In the present vogue of psychiatry, individual mental processes and behavior have been elaborately studied. Psychiatry for a nation, however, is still in embryo, though it is much the fashion to have discussions of mass behaviorism, public opinion, pressure groups, thought patterns, and propaganda. Scholars in the field of history tend more and more to speak in terms of culture; this often is represented as a matter of cultural conflict, as of German against Slav, of Japanese against Chinese, and the like. Such concepts were given overemphasis at the meeting of the American Historical Association last December [1939]. Historians are doing their age a disservice if these factors of culture are carried over, as they often are, whether by historians or others, into justifications or "explanations" of war. The note of caution here should be a note of honest inquiry. It may be seriously doubted whether war rises from fundamental motives of culture or economics so much as from the lack of cultural restraint or economic inhibition upon militaristic megalomania [delusions of greatness]. Modern wars do not relieve population pressure. Whether wars are . . . [needed] for economic outlets or for obtaining raw materials is highly doubtful. International trade brings all that. Those who create war throttle the very flow of trade that would promote economic objectives. Where the economy of a nation hinges upon an export market, it may happen that plotters of war in that nation will stupidly kill that market by devices of economic autarchy and then claim that they have to go to war to have trade outlets. It is the same with incoming goods. Of such is the economic argument for war. War makers do not open up economic benefit so much as they stifle it. Their relation to culture is no better than their relation to economy.

There is the word astrology for bogus astronomy and alchemy for false chemistry. Ought there not to be some such word for the economic alchemists of this world? Perhaps it exists in the word autarchy. Is it not in the category of bogus economics, or *ersatz* [substitute] economics, that one should put those who study war as a matter of trade, supply, resources, needs, and production? As for the Civil War the stretch and span of conscious economic motive was much smaller than the areas or classes of war involvement. Economic diversity offered as much motive for union, in order to have a well rounded nation, as for the kind of economic conflict suggested by secession. One fault of writers who associate war-making with economic advantage is false or defective economics; another is the historical fault. It is surprising how seldom the economic explanation of war has made its case historically, *i.e.* in terms of adequate historical evidence bearing upon those points and those minds where actually the plunge into war occurred. One hears war treated as a matter of culture, but cultural and racial consciousness are as strong in Scandinavia or the Netherlands or Switzerland as in militarist-ridden countries. To make conquest a matter of culture is poor history. It may be the vanquished whose culture survives. Culture is not easily transplanted if force be the method. When war comes by the violence of a few in control and by the stifling of economic and cultural processes, it ill becomes the scholar to add his piping to the cacophonous blare of militaristic propaganda. . . .

War-making is too much dignified if it is told in terms of broad national urges, of great German motives, or of compelling Russian ambitions. When nations stumble into war, or when peoples rub their eyes and find they have been dragged into war, there is at some point a psychopathic case. Omit the element of abnormality, or of bogus leadership, or inordinate ambition for conquest, and diagnosis fails. In the modern scene it fails also if one omits manipulation, dummies, bogeys, false fronts, provocative agents, made-up incidents, frustration of elemental impulses, negation of culture, propaganda that is false in intent, criminal usurpation, and terrorist violence. These are reflections on the present bedeviled age, but their pertinence to the subject at hand is seen in the fact that scholarly discussions in explanation of war on the economic or cultural basis frequently include the Civil War as a supposedly convincing example. The writer doubts seriously whether a consensus of scholars who have competently studied the Civil War would accept either the cultural motive or the economic basis as the effective cause. . . .

In writing of human nature in politics Graham Wallas [an English political scientist] has shown the potent effect of irrational attitudes. He might have found many a Civil War example. None of the "explanations" of the war make sense, if fully analyzed. The war has been "explained" by the choice of a Republican president, by grievances, by sectional economics, by the cultural wish for southern independence, by slavery, or by events at Sumter. But these explanations crack when carefully examined. The election of Lincoln fell so far short of swinging southern sentiment against the Union that secessionists were still unwilling to trust their case to an all-southern convention or to cooperation among southern states. In every election from 1840 to 1852 Lincoln voted for the same candidate for whom many thousands of southerners voted. Lincoln deplored the demise of the Whig party and would have been only too glad to have voted in 1856 for another Harrison, another Taylor, or another Fillmore. Alexander Stephens [Vice-president of the Confederacy] stated that secessionists did not desire redress of grievances and would obstruct such redress. Prophets of sectional economics left many a southerner unconvinced; it is doubtful how far their arguments extended beyond the sizzling pages of *DeBow's Review* and the agenda of southern commercial congresses. The tariff was a potential future annoyance rather than an acute grievance in 1860. What existed then was largely a southern tariff law. Practically all tariffs are one-sided. Sectional tariffs in other periods have existed without producing war. Southern independence on broad cultural lines is probably more of a modern thesis than a contemporary motive of sufficient force to have carried the South out of the Union on any cooperative, all-southern basis.

It was no part of the Republican program to smash slavery in the South, nor did the territorial aspect of slavery mean much politically beyond agitation. Southerners cared little about actually taking slaves into existing territories; Republicans cared so little in the opposite sense that they avoided the prohibition of slavery in those territorial laws that were passed with Republican votes in February and March, 1861. Things said of "the South" often failed to apply to southerners, or of "the North" to northerners. Thwarted "Southern rights" were more often a sublimation than a definite entity. "The North" in the militant pre-war sense was largely an abstraction. The Sumter affair was not a cause, but an incident resulting from pre-existing governmental deadlock; Sumter requires explanation, and that explanation carries one back into all the other alleged factors. In contemporary southern comments on Lincoln's course at Sumter one finds not harmony but a jangling of discordant voices. Virginia resented Lincoln's action at Sumter for a reason opposite to that of South Carolina; Virginia's resentment was in the anti-secessionist sense. By no means did all the North agree with Lincoln's course as to Sumter. Had Lincoln evacuated Sumter without an expedition, he would have been supported by five and a half of seven cabinet members, [Salmon] Chase taking a halfway stand and [Montgomery] Blair alone taking a positive stand for an expedition. What Lincoln refused as to Sumter was what the United States government had permitted in general as to forts and arsenals in the South. Stronger action than at Sumter was taken by Lincoln at Pickens without southern fireworks. There is no North-versus-South pattern that covers the subject of the forts. Nor is the war itself to be glibly explained in rational North-versus-South terms.

Let one take all the factors—the Sumter maneuver, the election of Lincoln, abolitionism, slavery in Kansas, cultural and economic differences—and it will be seen that only by a kind of false display could any of these issues, or all of them together, be said to have caused the war if one omits the elements of emotional unreason and overbold leadership.

If one word or phrase were selected to account for the war, that word would not be slavery, or state-rights, or diverse civilizations. It would have to be such a word as fanaticism (on both sides), or misunderstanding, or perhaps politics. To Graham Wallas misunderstanding and politics are the same thing.

The fundamental or the elemental is often no better than a philosophical will o' the wisp. Why do adventitious things, or glaringly abnormal things, have to be elementally or cosmically accounted for? If, without proving his point, the historian makes war a thing of "inevitable" economic conflict, or cultural expression, or *Lebensraum* [living space], his generalizations are caught up by others, for it would seem that those historians who do the most generalizing, if they combine effective writing with it, are the ones who are most often quoted. The historian's pronouncements are taken as the statement of laws whether he means them so or not; he is quoted by sociologists, psychologists, behaviorists, misbehaviorists, propagandists, and what not; he becomes a contributor to those "dynamic" masses of ideas, or ideologies, which are among the sorriest plagues of the present age. As to wars, the ones that have not happened are perhaps best to study. Much could be said about such wars. As much could be said in favor of them as of actual wars. Cultural and economic difficulties in wars that have not occurred are highly significant. The notion that you must have war when you have cultural variation, or economic competition, or sectional difference is an unhistorical misconception which it is stupid in historians to promote. Yet some of the misinterpretations of the Civil War have tended to promote it.

PROBLEM 9

The Civil War
as a Moral Crisis

It is easy to understand how the disasters of the twentieth century have led to a revulsion against war. It is also understandable why some people have concluded that perhaps man has been too sentimental and foolishly optimistic about the future. History furnishes overwhelming evidence that man often acts with cruelty and malice and that a strong irrational current belies a simple faith in progress.

This point of view has been expressed effectively, not by an historian but by a theologian, Reinhold Niebuhr. His writings emphasize the reality of evil, the limited capacities of man, and man's need for moral action. He criticizes those persons who believe in easy solutions to social and political problems.

Among other spokesmen for this belief is a small group of historians who are the modern counterparts of writers—especially Northern writers—of the Civil War generation who wrote in moralistic terms about the evils of human bondage. This renewed emphasis on the moral dimension of the slavery issue appeared at about the same time that interest in the guarantee of civil rights to American Negroes was rising to the highest point since Reconstruction days. The connection was probably more than simple coincidence.

Notable among the new moralists who have leveled their primary attack against the "blundering generation" thesis are Arthur M. Schlesinger, Jr., Bernard De Voto, and Pieter Geyl, a Dutch historian. They argue that blindness to the moral implications of slavery renders the revisionists incapable of understanding the intense emotionalism of the Civil War period.

Schlesinger cautions the historian against handing out moral judgments indiscriminately, but he insists that human slavery was uniquely and plainly wicked. The historian who ignores this truth, he warns, fails to account for the necessity of a moral decision in the face of a plainly recognizable wrong. The historian cannot simply wish that the Civil War had not happened, he cannot simply regret that there were abolitionists, or bemoan the dreadful bloodshed of the war. The facts are that the war was fought, there were zealots, deep passions, and bloodshed, and the historian must account for them. The new moralists do not propose a fatalistic resignation to the obvious wrongs of society. Rather, they urge "the necessity for decision and for struggle" to counter man's clearly demonstrated frailties and limitations.

These ideas have further muddied the waters of Civil War interpretation. The revisionists have faced this challenge without losing their large following among historians. Yet the new moralists, echoing in modern terms a theme common to the Civil War generation, have stimulated historians to reconsider moral factors in history.

In the reading that follows, Schlesinger attacks the thesis of the revisionists and defends the argument that moral considerations were significant in causing the Civil War.

As you read, consider these questions:

1   What evaluations do you believe Schlesinger would make of the economic and cultural explanations of the coming of the Civil War?

2   Schlesinger questions whether slavery would have disappeared without a war. Is he saying that immorality can be overcome only by violence?

3   Is the explanation of the Civil War as an "irrepressible conflict" the same as Schlesinger's moral causation?

4   Would you agree with Schlesinger that the struggle over extension of slavery into the territories was basically a moral issue?

5   Is Schlesinger mainly interested in attacking the revisionist attitude toward causes of the Civil War or does he have a further purpose?

6   Schlesinger indicates that the reaction to extension of slavery in the 1850's was similar to the reaction to Adolf Hitler's conquests in the 1930's. How does Schlesinger use this comparison to attack the revisionist thesis?

ETHICAL CONSIDERATIONS

Arthur Schlesinger, Jr., a Northern-bred liberal, said, "We delude ourselves when we think that history teaches us that evil will be 'outmoded' by progress." In the selection that follows, Schlesinger discusses the great moral dilemma of the Civil War. □ Arthur M. Schlesinger, Jr., "The Causes of the Civil War: A Note on Historical Sentimentalism." New York: *Partisan Review,* October 1949, pp. 969–981. Used by permission of Arthur M. Schlesinger, Jr.

The Civil War was our great national trauma. A savage fraternal conflict, it released deep sentiments of guilt and remorse—sentiments which have reverberated through our history and our literature ever since. Literature in the end came to terms with these sentiments by yielding to the South in fantasy the victory it had been denied in fact; this tendency culminated on the popular level in *Gone with the Wind* [a novel by Margaret Mitchell, published in 1936] . . . . But history, a less malleable medium, was constricted by the intractable fact that the war had taken place, and by the related assumption that it was, in William H. Seward's phrase, an "irrepressible conflict," and hence a justified one.

As short a time ago as 1937, for example, even Professor James G. Randall could describe himself as "unprepared to go to the point of denying that the great American tragedy could have been avoided." Yet in a few years the writing of history would succumb to the psychological imperatives which had produced *I'll Take my Stand* [a discussion of the South and the agrarian tradition by twelve Southerners, published in 1930] and *Gone with the Wind*; and Professor Randall would emerge as the leader of a triumphant new school of self-styled "revisionists." The publication of two vigorous books by Professor Avery Craven—*The Repressible Conflict* (1939) and *The Coming of the Civil War* (1942)—and the appearance of Professor Randall's own notable volumes on Lincoln—*Lincoln the President: Springfield to Gettysburg* (1945), *Lincoln and the South* (1946), and *Lincoln the Liberal Statesman* (1947)—brought about a profound reversal of the professional historian's attitude toward the Civil War. Scholars now denied the traditional assumption of the inevitability of the war and boldly advanced the thesis that a "blundering generation" had transformed a "repressible conflict" into a "needless war."

The swift triumph of revisionism came about with very little resistance or even expressed reservations on the part of the profession. Indeed, the only adequate evaluation of the revisionist thesis that I know was made, not by an academic historian at all, but by that illustrious semi-pro, Mr. Bernard De Voto [an editor and writer]; and Mr. De Voto's two brilliant articles in *Harper's* in 1945 unfortunately had little influence within the guild. . . .

This new interpretation surely deserves at least as meticulous an examination as Professor Randall is prepared to give. . . . The following notes are presented in the interests of stimulating such an examination.

The revisionist case, as expounded by Professors Randall and Craven, has three main premises. First:

1) that the Civil War was caused by the irresponsible emotionalization of politics far out of proportion to the real problems involved. The war, as Randall put it, was certainly not caused by cultural variations nor by economic rivalries nor by sectional differences; these all existed, but it was "stupid," as he declared, to think that they required war as a solution. . . .

Nor was the slavery the cause. The issues arising over slavery were in Randall's judgment "highly artificial, almost fabricated. . . . They produced quarrels out of things that would have settled themselves were it not for political agitation." Slavery, Craven observed, was in any case a much over-rated problem. It is "perfectly clear," he wrote, "that slavery played a rather minor part in the life of the South and of the Negro." . . .

If uncontrolled emotionalism and fanaticism caused the war, how did they get out of hand? Who whipped up the "whipped-up crisis"? Thus the second revisionist thesis:

2) that sectional friction was permitted to develop into needless war by the inexcusable failure of political leadership in the fifties. "It is difficult to achieve a full realization of how Lincoln's generation stumbled into a ghastly war," wrote Randall. ". . . If one questions the term 'blundering generation,' let him inquire how many measures of the time he would wish copied or repeated if the period were to be approached with a clean slate and to be lived again." . . .

. . . But if the indictment "blundering generation" meant no more than a general complaint that democratic politics placed a premium on emotionalism, then the Civil War would have been no more nor less "needless" than any event in our blundering history. The phrase "blundering generation" must consequently imply that the generation in power in the fifties was *below* the human or historical or democratic average in its blundering. Hence the third revisionist thesis:

3) that the slavery problem could have been solved without war. For, even if slavery were as unimportant as the revisionists have insisted, they would presumably admit that it constituted the real sticking-point in the relations between the sections. They must show therefore that there were policies with which a non-blundering generation could have resolved the

slavery crisis and averted war; and that these policies were so obvious that the failure to adopt them indicated blundering and stupidity of a peculiarly irresponsible nature. If no such policies could be produced even by hindsight, then it would seem excessive to condemn the politicians of the fifties for failing to discover them at the time.

The revisionists have shown only a most vague and sporadic awareness of this problem. "Any kind of sane policy in Washington in 1860 might have saved the day for nationalism," remarked Craven; but he did not vouchsafe the details of these sane policies; we would be satisfied to know about one. Similarly Randall declared that there were few policies of the fifties he would wish repeated if the period were to be lived over again; but he was not communicative about the policies he would wish pursued. Nevins likewise blamed the war on the "collapse of American statesmanship," but restrained himself from suggesting how a non-collapsible statesmanship would have solved the hard problems of the fifties. . . .

If, then, revisionism has rested on the assumption that the nonviolent abolition of slavery was possible, such abolition could conceivably have come about through internal reform in the South; through economic exhaustion of the slavery system in the South; or through some government project for gradual and compensated emancipation. Let us examine these possibilities.

1) *The internal reform argument.* The South, the revisionists have suggested, might have ended the slavery system, if left to its own devices; only the abolitionists spoiled everything by letting loose a hysteria which caused the southern ranks to close in self-defense.

This revisionist argument would have been more convincing if the decades of alleged antislavery feeling in the South had produced any concrete results. As one judicious southern historian, Professor Charles S. Sydnor, recently [1948] put it, "Although the abolition movement was followed by a decline of antislavery sentiment in the South, it must be remembered that in all the long years before that movement began no part of the South had made substantial progress toward ending slavery. . . . Southern liberalism had not ended slavery in any state."

In any case, it is difficult for historians seriously to suppose that northerners could have denied themselves feelings of disapproval over slavery. To say that there "should" have been no abolitionists in America before the Civil War is about as sensible as to say that there "should" have been no anti-Nazis in the nineteen-thirties or that there "should" be no anti-Communists today. People who indulge in criticism of remote evils may not be so pure of heart as they imagine; but that fact does not affect their inevitability as part of the historic situation.

Any theory, in short, which expects people to repress such spontaneous aversions is profoundly unhistorical. If revisionism has based itself on the conviction that things would have been different if only there had been no abolitionists, it has forgotten that abolitionism was as definite and irrevocable a factor in the historic situation as was slavery itself. And, just as abolitionism was inevitable, so too was the southern reaction against it—a reaction which, as Professor Clement Eaton has ably shown, steadily drove the free discussion of slavery out of the South. The extinction of free discussion meant, of course, the absolute extinction of any hope of abolition through internal reform.

2) *The economic exhaustion argument.* Slavery, it has been pointed out, was on the skids economically. It was overcapitalized and inefficient; it immobilized both capital and labor; its one-crop system was draining the soil of fertility; it stood in the way of industrialization. As the South came to realize these facts, a revisionist might argue, it would have moved to abolish slavery for its own economic good. As Craven put it, slavery "may have been almost ready to break down of its own weight."

This argument assumed, of course, that southerners would have recognized the causes of their economic predicament and taken the appropriate measures. Yet such an assumption would be plainly contrary to history and to experience. From the beginning the South has always blamed its economic shortcomings, not on its own economic ruling class and its own inefficient use of resources, but on northern exploitation. Hard times in the eighteen-fifties produced in the South, not a reconsideration of the slavery system, but blasts against the North for the high prices of manufactured goods. The overcapitalization of slavery led, not to criticisms of the system, but to increasingly insistent demands for the reopening of the slave trade. Advanced southern writers like George Fitzhugh and James D. B. DeBow were even arguing that slavery was adapted to industrialism. When Hinton R. Helper did advance before the Civil War an early version of Craven's argument, asserting that emancipation was necessary to save the southern economy, the South burned his book. Nothing in the historical record suggests that the southern ruling class was preparing to deviate from its traditional pattern of self-exculpation [that is, freeing itself from blame] long enough to take such a drastic step as the abolition of slavery.

3) *Compensated emancipation.* Abraham Lincoln made repeated proposals of compensated emancipation. In his annual message to Congress of December 1, 1862, he set forth a detailed plan by which States, on

an agreement to abolish slavery by 1900, would receive government bonds in proportion to the number of slaves emancipated. Yet, even though Lincoln's proposals represented a solution of the problem conceivably gratifying to the slaveholder's purse as well as to his pride, they got nowhere. . . .

Where have the revisionists gone astray? In part, the popularity of revisionism obviously parallels that of *Gone with the Wind*—the victors paying for victory by pretending literary defeat. But the essential problem is why history should be so vulnerable to this literary fashion; and this problem, I believe, raises basic questions about the whole modern view of history. It is perhaps stating the issue in too portentous terms. Yet I cannot escape the feeling that the vogue of revisionism is connected with the modern tendency to seek in optimistic sentimentalism an escape from the severe demands of moral decision; that it is the offspring of our modern sentimentality which at once evades the essential moral problems in the name of a superficial objectivity and asserts their unimportance in the name of an invincible progress.

The revisionists first glided over the implications of the fact that the slavery system was producing a closed society in the South. . . .

. . . No society, I suppose, encourages criticism of its basic institutions. Yet, when a democratic society acts in self-defense, it does so at least in the name of human dignity and freedom. When a society based on bond slavery acts to eliminate criticism of its peculiar institution, it outlaws what a believer in democracy can only regard as the abiding values of man. When the basic institutions are evil, in other words, the effect of attempts to defend their existence can only be the moral and intellectual stultification of the society.

A society closed in the defense of evil institutions thus creates moral differences far too profound to be solved by compromise. Such a society forces upon every one, both those living at the time and those writing about it later, the necessity for a moral judgment; and the moral judgment in such cases becomes an indispensable factor in the historical understanding. . . .

Because the revisionists felt no moral urgency themselves, they deplored as fanatics those who did feel it, or brushed aside their feelings as the artificial product of emotion and propaganda. The revisionist hero was Stephen A. Douglas, who always thought that the great moral problems could be solved by sleight-of-hand. The phrase "northern man of southern sentiments," Randall remarked, was "said opprobriously . . . as if it were a base thing for a northern man to work with his southern fellows."

By denying themselves insight into the moral dimension of the slavery crisis, in other words, the revisionists denied themselves a historical understanding of the intensities that caused the crisis. It was the moral issue of slavery, for example, that gave the struggles over slavery in the territories or over the enforcement of the fugitive slave laws their significance. These issues, as the revisionists have shown with cogency, were not in themselves basic. But they were the available issues; they were almost the only points within the existing constitutional framework where the moral conflict could be faced; as a consequence, they became charged with the moral and political dynamism of the central issue. To say that the Civil War was fought over the "unreal" issue of slavery in the territories is like saying that the Second World War was fought over the "unreal" issue of the invasion of Poland. The democracies could not challenge fascism inside Germany any more than opponents of slavery could challenge slavery inside the South; but the extension of slavery, like the extension of fascism, was an act of aggression which made a moral choice inescapable.

Let us be clear what the relationship of moral judgment to history is. Every historian, as we all know in an argument that surely does not have to be repeated in 1949, imports his own set of moral judgments into the writing of history by the very process of interpretation; and the phrase "every historian" includes the category "revisionist." Mr. De Voto in his paraphrases of the revisionist position has put admirably the contradictions on this point: as for "moral questions, God forbid. History will not put itself in the position of saying that any thesis may have been wrong, any cause evil. . . . History will not deal with moral values, though of course the Republican radicals were, well, culpable." The whole revisionist attitude toward abolitionists and radicals, repeatedly characterized by Randall as "unctuous" and "intolerant," overflows with the moral feeling which is so virtuously excluded from discussions of slavery.

An acceptance of the fact of moral responsibility does not license the historian to roam through the past ladling out individual praise and blame: such an attitude would ignore the fact that all individuals, including historians, are trapped in a web of circumstance which curtails their moral possibilities. But it does mean that there are certain essential issues on which it is necessary for the historian to have a position if he is to understand the great conflicts of history. These great conflicts are relatively few because there are few enough historical phenomena which we can confidently identify as evil. The essential issues appear, moreover, not in pure and absolute form, but incomplete and imperfect, compromised by the deep complexity of history. Their proponents may often be neurotics and fanatics, like the abolitionists. They may attain a social importance only when a configuration of non-moral factors—economic, political, social, military—permit them to do so.

Yet neither the nature of the context nor the pretensions of the proponents alter the character of the issue. And human slavery is certainly one of the few issues of whose evil we can be sure. It is not just "a very ancient labor system"; it is also a betrayal of the basic values of our Christian and democratic tradition. No historian can understand the circumstances which led to its abolition until he writes about it in its fundamental moral context. "History is supposed to understand the difference between a decaying economy and an expanding one," as Mr. De Voto well said, "between solvency and bankruptcy, between a dying social idea and one coming to world acceptance. . . . It is even supposed to understand implications of the difference between a man who is legally a slave and one who is legally free."

"Revisionism in general has no position," De Voto continues, "but only a vague sentiment." Professor Randall well suggested the uncritical optimism of that sentiment when he remarked, "To suppose that the Union could not have been continued or slavery outmoded without the war and without the corrupt concomitants of war is hardly an enlightened assumption." We have here a touching afterglow of the admirable nineteenth-century faith in the full rationality and perfectibility of man; the faith that the errors of the world would all in time be "outmoded" (Professor Randall's use of this word is suggestive) by progress. Yet the experience of the twentieth century has made it clear that we gravely overrated man's capacity to solve the problems of existence within the terms of history.

This conclusion about man may disturb our complacencies about human nature. Yet it is certainly more in accord with history than Professor Randall's "enlightened" assumption that men can solve peaceably all the problems which overwhelm him. The unhappy fact is that man occasionally works himself into a log-jam; and that the log-jam must be burst by violence. We know that well enough from the experience of the last decade. Are we to suppose that some future historian will echo Professor Nevins' version of the "failure" of the eighteen-fifties and write: "The primary task of statesmanship in the nineteen-thirties was to furnish a workable adjustment between the United States and Germany, while offering strong inducements to the German people to abandon the police state and equal persuasions to the Americans to help the Nazis rather than scold them"? Will some future historian adapt Professor Randall's formula and write that the word "appeaser" was used "opprobriously" as if it were a "base" thing for an American to work with his Nazi fellow? Obviously this revisionism of the future (already foreshadowed in the work of Charles A. Beard) would represent, as we now see it, a fantastic evasion of the hard and unpleasant problems of the thirties. I doubt whether our present revisionism would make much more sense to the men of the eighteen-fifties.

The problem of the inevitability of the Civil War, of course, is in its essence a problem devoid of meaning. The revisionist attempt to argue that the war could have been avoided by "any kind of sane policy" is of interest less in its own right than as an expression of a characteristically sentimental conception of man and of history. And the great vogue of revisionism in the historical profession suggests, in my judgment, ominous weaknesses in the contemporary attitude toward history.

We delude ourselves when we think that history teaches us that evil will be "outmoded" by progress and that politics consequently does not impose on us the necessity for decision and for struggle. If historians are to understand the fullness of the social dilemma they seek to reconstruct, they must understand that sometimes there is no escape from the implaca-bilities of moral decision. When social conflicts embody great moral issues, these conflicts cannot be assigned for solution to the invincible march of progress; nor can they be bypassed with "objective" neutrality. Not many problems perhaps force this decision upon the historian. But, if any problem does in our history, it is the Civil War.

To reject the moral actuality of the Civil War is to foreclose the possibility of an adequate account of its causes. More than that, it is to misconceive and grotesquely to sentimentalize the nature of history. For history is not a redeemer, promising to solve all human problems in time; nor is man capable of transcending the limitations of his being. Man generally is entangled in insoluble problems; history is consequently a tragedy in which we are all involved, whose keynote is anxiety and frustration, not progress and fulfillment. Nothing exists in history to assure us that the great moral dilemmas can be resolved without pain; we cannot therefore be relieved from the duty of moral judgment on issues so appalling and inescapable as those involved in human slavery; nor can we be consoled by sentimental theories about the needlessness of the Civil War into regarding our own struggles against evil as equally needless.

One must emphasize, however, that this duty of judgment applies to issues. Because we are all implicated in the same tragedy, we must judge the men of the past with the same forbearance and charity which we hope the future will apply toward us.

PROBLEM 10

The Civil War: A Survey

Unit Two has presented four interpretations of the causes of the Civil War. They include the economic view, the conflict of cultures thesis, the revisionist argument that the war was "needless," and the emphasis on the moral issue of slavery as a center of causative considerations.

Each point of view has been endorsed by some historians and each has been rejected by others. For example, Avery Craven is in substantial agreement with James G. Randall's revisionist argument, though his emphasis differs; Pieter Geyl, a Dutch historian, supports the arguments of Arthur M. Schlesinger, Jr., who criticized the revisionists.

In the reading for Problem 10, David M. Potter, Coe professor of history at Stanford University, reviews the interpretations considered in this volume and presents some new views. A careful reading of the five Problems should give the student some knowledge of the major interpretations, but merely knowing the hypotheses is not enough. If he is to progress in skillful analysis, the student should follow the suggestion which Potter makes in the last sentence of his essay. After carefully examining the facts and leading interpretations, the student should come to his own conclusions concerning the record of the past. In so doing he is developing a philosophy of history in the same manner as the professional writers represented in this book.

As you read, consider the following questions:

1   Is there any similarity between interpretations of the causes of the American Revolution and of the Civil War? Does a study of the causes of the Revolution help explain the coming of the Civil War?

2   How do you account for the continuing disagreement among historians about the causes of the Civil War?

3   Is there such a thing as historical truth? If so, how can it be recognized?

4   David M. Potter was born and educated in the South. Does the excerpt in Problem 10 indicate his own philosophical view or bias?

5   Which of the interpretations in this unit is most convincing to you?

THE BACKGROUND OF THE CIVIL WAR

Laying particular stress on the revisionist and anti-revisionist interpretations, David M. Potter analyzes modern scholarship dealing with the origins of the Civil War. □ David M. Potter, "The Background of the Civil War," *Interpreting and Teaching American History*, Thirty-first Yearbook of the National Council for the Social Studies, pp. 88–90, 91–98, 118–119. Washington, D.C.: National Council for the Social Studies, 1961.

The last twenty years have witnessed considerable advances in the historical understanding of many of the developments which preceded the Civil War, but it can hardly be said that they have brought us visibly closer to the point at which a jury of historians seems likely to arrive at a verdict which will settle the controversy as to causes. Indeed some of the most fundamental issues in the controversy, namely those turning upon the significance of the slavery question, have been reactivated and seem now to leave the dispute farther from settlement than ever.

By 1940, the literature on the Civil War had already been accumulating for eighty years.[1] During these eight decades, interpretation of the War had passed through three major phases. First, during the immediate post-war era, there had been a literature by participants and partisans, de-

---

[1] Efforts to explain the War in historical terms began as early as 1861–62, with interpretations by John L. Motley, George Bancroft, Francis Parkman, and Edward A. Pollard. For general discussion of the historiography of the War, including these writers, see Thomas J. Pressly, *Americans Interpret Their Civil War* (Princeton: Princeton University, 1954) and Howard K. Beale, "What Historians Have Said About the Causes of the Civil War," in Social Science Research Council Bulletin 54, *Theory and Practice in Historical Study* (New York: Social Science Research Council, 1946).—*David M. Potter.*

signed to justify their own course of conduct and therefore striving either to vindicate or indict. Both sides had appealed to absolute values: if they were partisans of the Union, they had explained the War in terms of slavery and disunion, appealing to the moral absolute of human freedom and national unity; if they were partisans of the South, they had explained it in terms of the secession issue, appealing to the legal absolute inherent in the theory of state sovereignty and to the moral absolute of the right of self-government.

Second, in the period after the wounds of war began to heal, there had been a nationalistic interpretation, well exemplified in the seven-volume history by James Ford Rhodes (1893–1906), which avoided the attribution of blame and emphasized the sincerity and high motive of both the Blue and the Gray. Rhodes himself argued unequivocally that slavery was the cause of the War, but he held the nation rather than the South responsible for slavery, and if he blamed the South for secession, he blamed the North for Reconstruction. In such an interpretation the concept of an inevitable or "irrepressible" conflict fitted well, for if the War could not possibly have been prevented, then no one could be blamed for failing to prevent it, and thus no one was guilty. Charles Francis Adams [an American lawyer, diplomat, and author] pushed this view to its logical limit in 1902 by declaring that "Everybody, in short, was right; no one wrong."

Third, in the 1920's, after ideas of economic determinism began to prevail widely in American intellectual circles, Charles and Mary Beard had published an immensely influential interpretation of the War in their *The Rise of American Civilization.* Seeing the great contests of history as struggles for power, rather than for principle, and regarding moral and legal arguments as mere rationalizations, the Beards had denied that the South really cared about states rights or the North about slavery. The South had simply used states rights as a tactical device in defending a minority position. The Republicans had simply used the slavery issue to turn public opinion against the South, but in fact the Republicans had not been abolitionists and had done nothing to help the slaves, but had sought only to "contain" the power of the slaveholders by excluding them from the new territories. The War, therefore, had not been a contest over principles but a struggle for power—a clash of economic sections in which freedom did not necessarily combat slavery but industrialism most assuredly combated the planter interests.

These three were, in brief, the major interpretations which had held sway up to 1940. Since 1940, the major tendencies have been: (1) the development of a so-called "revisionist" interpretation which minimized the importance of slavery or any other fundamental factor as a cause of the War and also argued that the War could have been and should have been averted;

and (2) a counterattack upon the revisionists by writers who reassert the causative importance of the slavery question.

Although sometimes mentioned as if they were a "school," the so-called revisionists have in fact been a number of distinctively independent scholars, working separately, disagreeing on occasion, and united only by their skepticism about the role of slavery as the heart of the sectional issue and their doubt that the conflict was irrepressible.

These doubts are as old as the War itself, but modern revisionism possibly begins with Albert J. Beveridge, Republican Senator from Indiana and biographer of John Marshall. About 1920, Beveridge set out to write a biography of Lincoln. He approached this undertaking with the traditional Republican reverence for an almost superhuman being—the inevitable protagonist of the anti-slavery drama in which there had to be an antagonist or villain, and in which Stephen A. Douglas was inevitably stereotyped for the latter role. But when Beveridge began his research, he found the facts far more complex than the tradition, and when he came to the Lincoln-Douglas debates, he concluded that Douglas had acted with integrity and had represented a very respectable point of view—namely that the question of slavery in the territories was a fictitious issue, not worth a crisis which would endanger the nation. Because the abolitionists had "agitated" this issue in such a way as to precipitate the crisis, Beveridge formed an unfavorable opinion of them and began to think that, without them, there might have been no war—indeed that slavery might in time have disappeared peaceably under the pressure of economic forces. . . .

. . . [The] full tide of the revisionist reaction struck in the late thirties and early forties, primarily as the result of the work of two men—James G. Randall and Avery O. Craven—advancing independently along somewhat parallel lines.

Craven first enunciated his views clearly in an article, "Coming of the War Between the States: An Interpretation," in 1936. He followed this with a brief interpretive volume, *The Repressible Conflict,* in 1939, and with a full scale history of the years from 1830 to 1861 in *The Coming of the Civil War* in 1942. Since then he has continued to develop and to modify his ideas in a number of writings, including notably a volume on *The Growth of Southern Nationalism, 1848–1861* (1953) in the History of the South Series, and a set of interpretive lectures, *Civil War in the Making, 1815–1860* (1959).

Perhaps the crucial feature of Craven's interpretation is his belief that the basic and essential differences between North and South were not great enough to make war necessary. The dissimilarities between the agrarian society of the South and the industrial society of the Northeast were, to be sure, a fertile seed-bed for friction and for misunderstandings, but these misunderstandings were not, on the whole, realistic. The great difference traditionally emphasized is that of slavery, but Craven argued that the economic condition of the Negro as an unskilled laborer engaged in the cotton culture was much more important in controlling the conditions of his life than his legal status as a chattel. Because of these economic factors the condition of the Negro after emancipation changed very little until the cotton economy itself changed in the 1930's. Craven also emphasized the fact that three-quarters of the Southern whites were not slaveholders and were not directly involved in the slavery complex. North and South did not, in fact, present polar extremes.

But if sectional antagonisms did not arise out of fundamental differences, what did they arise from? Craven believed that they resulted from the creation of false images of each section by the other, and from the charging of these images with a high, unreasoning emotional content. He believed that these stereotypes were to some extent manufactured by irresponsible political agitators, both North and South—that is by the "fire eating" secessionists and by the abolitionists. In other words, the explanation lies more in psychological attitudes than in objective conditions. From this conclusion, it follows that we should beware of any arbitrary assumption that the conflict was irrepressible (though Craven later concluded that the opposite assumption should also be avoided, since the question really cannot be determined). It follows, too, that slavery should be played down: Craven suggested "the possibility that behind the determination to put slavery on the road to ultimate extinction, there may have lain drives that had little to do with Negro slavery or the American South, as well as others that were the direct product of slavery itself and of the so-called 'Slave Power'." Since, in his opinion, "the great body of Americans were moderate and conservative in their attitudes (and) . . . came to the brink of Civil War reluctantly," a heavy burden of what may really be called war-guilt rests with the political leaders ("extremists") like Charles Sumner [Senator from Massachusetts] and [Robert] Barnwell Rhett [Southern writer] who played upon public emotions until they brought about a conflict which the circumstances did not require and which neither the Northern nor the Southern majority wanted.

While Craven was developing these themes at the University of Chicago, James G. Randall at the University of Illinois was concurrently working out an intepretation to which he himself applied the term "revisionist." His first clear-cut statement of this interpretation appeared, but was not heavily emphasized, in his *The Civil War and Reconstruction* in 1937. It was more fully elaborated in three important articles, "The Blundering Generation," "The

Civil War Restudied," and "When War Came in 1861," all published in 1940. Finally, in *Lincoln, the President: Springfield to Gettysburg* (1945), he set forth his views in their fully matured form.

Critics sometimes discuss Craven and Randall as if their views were identical. It is easy to see why this happens, for both men held a number of major ideas in common: that sectional differences were not great enough to necessitate a war; that the crisis resulted more from the whipping-up of emotions than from the impact of realistic issues; that extremists on both sides were responsible for this emotional jag, but that the responsibility of the extremists of the North (i.e., the abolitionists) which had been disregarded by many historians, needed to be emphasized rather more than the responsibility of the extremists of the South (i.e., the fire-eating secessionists) whom historians had blamed excessively; and above all, that the War was both avoidable and unnecessary and that it occurred as the result of a failure of leadership. But within this broad framework of agreement, Craven and Randall each developed distinctive points of emphasis. Where Craven argued that the Civil War in particular ought not to have occurred, Randall showed greater concern with the problem of war as such, and writing at a time when the world was rapidly losing the international peace which World War I and the League of Nations were supposed to have won, he argued that war as such should be prevented, that it is a "fallacy" to believe that "fundamental motives produce war." Indeed, he contended that analysis of the causes of war must fail unless it takes into consideration psychopathic factors.

Because of his greater concern with the general problem of the causation of war, Randall was also more concerned than was Craven to refute the idea of economic determinism in the Beardian sense, as an explanation of war. In some of his best analysis, Randall pointed out that economic determinists have a kind of "heads, I win—tails, you lose" formula. If a people who lack economic diversity make war, their belligerence can be explained in terms of the need for economic self-sufficiency. But if a people with diversity have an internal war, their conflict can be explained in terms of the clash of diverse interests. In either case, the explanation for war stands ready-made. As Randall argued, features of diversity may lead to mutual interdependence rather than to war, and the existence of economic differences creates no presumption that antagonism need follow. Where antagonism exists, it must be explained on specific grounds.

A second respect in which Randall's emphasis differed from Craven's is that where Craven discounted the significance of slavery as an institution, Randall minimized its significance as an issue. One of his most effective arguments was his contention that, while the broad issue of freedom versus slavery may be worth a war, the issue as defined by the opposing forces in 1861 was not that broad, and was not worth a war in the form in which they defined it; for the Republicans in 1861 did not propose to emancipate the slaves, they even agreed in 1861 to guarantee slavery in the existing slave states and to return fugitives to slavery. The one point on which they stuck was that they would not sanction slavery in any of the new territories. But since the climate and the economy of these new regions made them inhospitable to slavery anyway, the territorial question could be viewed as an abstraction—a contest over "an imaginary Negro in an impossible place," and a very inadequate cause for a war. The idea that the territorial issue was a fictitious one was not new—it had been vigorously expressed by James K. Polk—but Randall gave it a new application in his treatment of the causes of war.

A third major expression of revisionism appeared in 1948, when Roy F. Nichols of the University of Pennsylvania published his *The Disruption of American Democracy*. Unlike Craven and Randall, Nichols did not undertake a general interpretation of the sectional crisis as a whole. Instead he set himself to the more specialized study of the impact of sectional antagonisms in shattering a national political party—the Democratic party. His work, which won the Pulitzer Prize was, therefore, an institutional study of the impact of sectional pressures upon American political machinery. But the findings fitted well with the revisionist thesis, for Nichols showed how the defects of the political system (excessive localism, the need for agitation in order to stimulate voters in the frequent elections, etc.) contributed to the breakdown of a national political organization under the weight of sectional pressures. Moreover, Nichols asserted in clear-cut terms his belief that the "hyperemotionalism" of the times made it possible for "irresponsible and blind operators of local political machinery" to exploit the inflammable issues which led to war.

Toward the end of the forties, revisionism had very largely swept the field of Civil War literature. With the partial exception of Allan Nevins' *Ordeal of the Union* (1947), all the major works on the Civil War for a decade had reflected a revisionist view. Revisionism had made its way into the textbooks, and had been taken up by popular writers. It is perhaps symptomatic that, in 1951, William E. Woodward's posthumous history of the War, tentatively entitled: *The Civil War: A National Blunder,* was finally issued under the title, *Years of Madness.* [These titles are mentioned in Pressly, *Americans Interpret their Civil War,* p. 285.]

About nine years after Craven and Randall had sounded the first trumpets of a broad revisionism, Arthur Schlesinger, Jr., in his *The Age of Jackson* (1945) entered a dissenting opinion. In a brief discussion, made in passing,

Schlesinger affirmed his belief that "the emotion which moved the North finally to battlefield and bloodshed was moral disgust with slavery." He also denied the Beardian thesis that slavery was resisted because it constituted an obstacle to industrial capitalism; on the contrary, he said, "the aspirations which were first felt to be menaced by the slave power were in actuality democratic aspirations." Four years later, in an article on Randall's contention he returned to the subject for a more extended treatment. Attacking the revisionists for using the claim of objectivity and the concept of automatic progress as devices for avoiding consideration of the moral issue of slavery, Schlesinger argued that the focus of the slavery contest had fallen on the territories, not because industrialists on-the-make were covetous of power in new regions and indifferent to slave hardships in old ones, but because Americans found their moral scruples about slavery in conflict with their civic scruples to obey the Constitution, which protected slavery in the slave states. Therefore, their powerful impulse against human bondage was deflected from its natural target, slavery in the states, and was sublimated, as it were, into an attack on the peripheral question of slavery in the territories. But despite this displacement of the objective, Schlesigner felt no doubt that the moral question of slavery was basic in precipitating conflict between the sections.

During the same year when Schlesinger published this latter article, Pieter Geyl, an eminent Dutch historian of major stature, also published, in Dutch, a critique of Randall's idea that the War could have been avoided. (A part of this was published in English translation in 1951). Geyl focused his attention especially on Randall's contention that because the majority did not want conflict, war should have been avoidable. He argued that the historical process is not as rational as Randall assumed, and that the issues of sectional disagreement could not be neatly separated from the emotions which they generated, and which ultimately got out of control. His criticism must rank with Schlesinger's as one of the two major rebuttals to the revisionist argument, but other voices have been raised as well. Bernard De Voto assailed the revisionists in two influential articles in *Harper's Magazine,* which were notable for their early date (1946) as well as for their vigorous, hard-hitting tone. In 1950, Oscar Handlin [an American historian and educator], in a review of Nevins, deplored the practice of equating the abolitionists and the secessionists because both groups were fanatics: "There is surely a difference," he said, "between being a fanatic for freedom and being a fanatic for slavery."

Harry V. Jaffa has provided an important full-scale criticism of much of the revisionist position. [*Crisis of the House Divided. An Interpretation of the Issues in the Lincoln-Douglas Debates* (New York: Doubleday, 1959)] Jaffa denied that slavery had reached the geographical limits of its expansion and that the political restriction was redundant. He denied also that Douglas' popular sovereignty and Lincoln's restrictionism would both have come to the same thing, that is freedom in the territories, and that they presented no basic issue. Instead he argued, Douglas was willing to sacrifice the principles of freedom and equality to the principle of majority rule, while Lincoln, though not a doctrinaire equalitarian, wanted "the highest degree of equality for which general [majority] consent could be obtained." Emphasizing this distinction as he did, he dismissed the idea that emotions of the crisis period were "whipped up" or unrealistic. Don E. Fehrenbacher [an American historian], moreover, showed how genuinely Lincoln feared that the Dred Scott decision was a prelude to steps which would legalize slavery throughout the nation, and how effectively Lincoln himself defined the fundamental incompatibility between his position and Douglas'. [Don E. Fehrenbacher, "The Origins and Purpose of Lincoln's House Divided Speech," *Mississippi Valley Historical Review,* 46:615–43; March 1960]

The counterattack upon revisionism has gained a wide following, perhaps because many historians felt dissatisfied with a revisionist version of history, and welcomed a challenge to it. But the critics of revisionism have not been specialists in the Civil War period: Schlesinger is an authority on the Jacksonian and New Deal periods; Geyl on Dutch history; Jaffa is a political scientist. Consequently, they have stated their views in critical essays but, with the exception of Jaffa, have not woven them into the fabric of historical narrative. Craven, Randall, and Nichols, by contrast, have been such diligent researchers and such prolific writers on the developments of the crisis period that many teachers who may disagree with their interpretations nevertheless rely upon their histories for content. With one capital exception, most of the general historical exposition during the last twenty years has been written by revisionists. This exception is Allan Nevins.

Many years ago, Nevins conceived the idea of a large scale history that would treat the entire period of sectional crisis and Civil War from 1850 to 1865. Since James Ford Rhodes, at the turn of the century, published his volumes on the period 1850–1877, no such history had been written by anyone, and certainly none such had been written in the light of modern historical scholarship. Nevins engaged in a vast research enterprise, and in 1947 he published two volumes [*Ordeal of the Union*] covering the period 1850–1857; two more [*The Emergence of Lincoln*] in 1950 carried the narrative to 1860; and a fifth [*The War for the Union*] in 1959 has covered the outbreak of war and the War itself to the end of 1861.

Some critics complain that Nevins did not apply a consistent philosophy in his interpretation of the crisis. At some times he seemed, like the revisionists, to emphasize "the unrealities of passion"; at others the view that "while hysteria was important, we have always to ask what basic reasons made possible the propaganda which aroused it." On the one hand he seemed to agree with the revisionists that "failure of American leadership" contributed to the breakdown of Union, and he even stated a belief that "the War should have been avoidable," which is by no means the same as saying that it could have been avoided. Also, he rejected the older simplistic idea that slavery as a moral issue was the crux of the controversy, and offered in its stead the view that "the main root of the conflict (and there were minor roots), was the problem of slavery *with its complementary problem of race-adjustment.* . . . It was a war over slavery *and* the future position of the Negro race in North America." But this view, itself, was far from a revisionist position, and Nevins rejected revisionism even more distinctly in his attention to the harsher aspects of slavery and in his condemnation of what he considered the moral obtuseness of Stephen A. Douglas in sponsoring the Kansas-Nebraska Act.

In the light of Nevins' treatment, one might infer that revisionism, like all historical correctives, has served its purpose not by winning adoption of its own categorical views, but by forcing a modification in the conventional themes. Never again can well-trained historians explain the Civil War purely in terms of economic determinism or of the moral crusade against slavery; never again can they dismiss questions of responsibility and failure of leadership with the blanket formula that the conflict was irrepressible. These are lasting consequences of revisionism.

But questions of the role of leadership, the role of psychological factors ("emotions"), and above all, the role of slavery, remain and perhaps will continue to remain the subject of debate. Abraham Lincoln, a master of exact statement, said in his second inaugural, "all know that slavery was somehow the cause of the war." The operative word was "somehow," and it is around this word that historical debate continues to turn. . . .

The literature on all the varied questions which impinge directly or indirectly upon the Civil War is so vast that it almost defies the effort to view it together in any one focus. Perhaps the most pervasive quality which it all has in common is that it continues to be explicitly or implicitly controversial. Not only have historians failed to agree as to whether slavery furnished the basic motive for the war or whether it provided a smoke-screen for concealing the basic motives; they have also disagreed as to the nature of the society of the Old South, the nature of slavery, the motivation and character of the anti-slavery movement, and the interpretation of every link in the chain of sectional clashes which preceded the final crisis. The irony of this disagreement lies in the fact that it persists in the face of vastly increased factual knowledge and constantly intensified scholarly research. The discrepancy, indeed, is great enough to make apparent a reality about history which is seldom so self-evident as it is here: namely that factual mastery of the data alone does not necessarily lead to agreement upon broad questions of historical truth. It certainly narrows the alternatives between which controversy continues to rage, and this narrowing of alternatives is itself an important proof of objective progress. But within the alternatives the determination of truth depends more perhaps upon basic philosophical assumptions which are applied in interpreting the data, than upon the data themselves. Data, in this sense, are but the raw materials for historical interpretation and not the determinants of the interpretive process. This is why the heavily researched field of the coming of the Civil War still remains, and seems likely ever to remain, subject to what we call reinterpretation—by which we mean the application of individual philosophical views to the record of the past.

unit three

World War I

The year 1964 marked the fiftieth anniversary of the start of World War I. Overshadowed by World War II, which began twenty-five years later, and other conflicts, the first "Great War" is fast receding into the past. Yet the earlier struggle so largely determined the tragic events which followed it that, as George F. Kennan, an American diplomat, said, "all lines of inquiry . . . lead back to it."

The readings in this third unit of *The Causes of War* explore the historical interpretations of the American entry into World War I. The half-century since 1918 became turbulent in both domestic and foreign affairs. The results of the war brought disillusionment to the twenties and a retreat from internationalism. In the thirties, Americans, bedeviled by a severe depression, exemplified this retreat as they lapsed into a spirit of isolationism. At the end of the thirties, World War II began. It raged for six years and was followed by the Cold War, which was no less frightful in its possible scope and consequences. Historians of World War I reflect the concerns of the hectic years that followed the conflict in their analyses of the causes of American intervention. This third unit presents four major interpretations: Problem 11 deals with the revisionist school. Convinced that American entry into war was a mistake, the revisionists blamed that act on bankers, munitions makers, and propagandists, and on weak politicians who succumbed to these pressure groups. The reading in Problem 12, by Charles Seymour, represents an effort to find factors on which President Woodrow Wilson based his recommendation for war. Problem 13 presents the case in favor of intervention in order to protect American security and to retain the military balance of power in the Western world. Largely a post-World War II viewpoint, this emphasis on security has grown as world conditions have increased a feeling of insecurity. The fourth interpretation, in Problem 14, suggests that Wilson and the American people acted emotionally and idealistically because they believed that German aggression was morally wrong. It suggests also that their attitude might be characterized as a concern for strengthening the moral power in the world.

Historians of World War I may be divided roughly into two groups. As Ernest May, in Problem 15, put it, they either ask "What happened?" or "What went wrong?" The what-happened approach encourages an objective study of the record. The what-went-wrong approach seeks enlightenment from history.

In using the first approach, historians have tended to examine not only events in America but also those in other countries. They have concluded that no country could control fully the actions of others and that the sequence of tragic events in World War I were unavoidable.

In using the second approach, historians have been inclined to make judgments about past actions to gain insights relevant to the present.

However, both approaches bring up an old historical problem. The first method runs the risk of putting historical writing into a moral vacuum by suspending judgment. On the other hand, to dispense judgment too freely leads to an overemphasis of what should or might have happened at the cost of paying too little attention to what did happen.

The historian has a primary commitment to examine the record as completely and objectively as he can. But the facts do not speak for themselves, and he must analyze them to ascertain their meaning. In doing so he should be aware that the questions he asks about the past are often colored by current problems, and he should avoid the temptation to impose the lessons of his own time on the events of an earlier day. The historian and the policy maker alike need to realize that historical figures —like men today—have always been limited by the difficulty of seeing very far into the future.

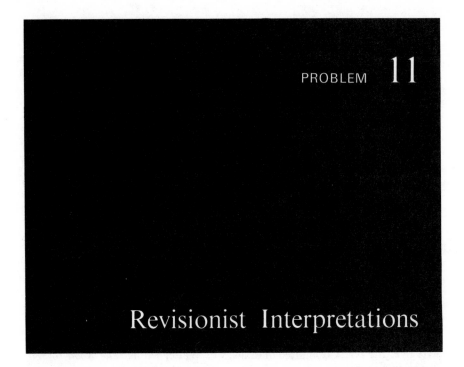

PROBLEM 11

Revisionist Interpretations

In a nation at war, powerful forces work to solidify public sentiment behind the war effort. Following the course of other belligerents, the government of the United States in 1917 promoted an official view of the purposes of the war and tried to minimize dissent. Most Americans had come to believe that the Great War, or World War I, was a struggle to protect Western democracy against the spread of German militarism, and many agreed with President Wilson when he called the conflict a war to "keep the world safe for democracy." The President's "peace without victory" speech of January 22, 1917, as well as his program for peace set forth in his "Fourteen Points" and presented to Congress on January 8, 1918, gave hope that the old cycle of one war begetting another would come to an end. Until the late 1920's most American historical writing reflected this viewpoint, expressing pride in American participation in a victory for peace and democracy.

This idealism changed to profound disillusionment in the late 1920's and continued into the 1930's.

Ironically, the war to "make the world safe for democracy" helped bring about the Bolshevik dictatorship in Russia. In the United States, the people were faced with the scandals of the Harding administration, the rise of the Ku Klux Klan, prohibition, the growth of organized crime, and a glorification of materialism.

Out of these distressing circumstances emerged a "revisionist" school of popular and professional historians which expressed the prevailing bitterness over the blighted hopes of Wilsonian idealism. Harry Elmer Barnes in his *Genesis of the World War* (1926) declared that American intervention had been a disaster. C. Hartley Grattan, who had been a student of Barnes, argued in his book *Why We Fought* (1929) that the United States went to war primarily because of economic ties with Allied powers, Allied propaganda, and inept diplomacy that imposed lower standards of neutrality on the Allies than it did on Germany.

Grattan's pioneer work influenced much of the later revisionist writing. In addition, the shock of the stock market crash in 1929 and the depression that followed, together with increasingly critical developments in Italy, Germany, and Manchuria, strengthened views that the war had been futile. The well-publicized Senate Munitions Investigating Committee of 1934–1936, headed by Senator Gerald P. Nye, stimulated an outpouring of books and articles which followed the revisionist line.

The most widely read revisionist book, appearing at the height of publicity over the Nye Committee findings, was Walter Millis' *The Road to War* (1935). This well-written, colorful account implied that propaganda and commercial ties were responsible for American intervention. By far the most scholarly revisionist study was Charles C. Tansill's *America Goes to War* (1938), an impressively documented and researched volume. Although Tansill cited many possible causes of American intervention, he emphasized President Wilson's failure to resist pressures from business interests and his strong stand on German submarine warfare.

The tendency among revisionist writers was to view all war as essentially wrong, and therefore that United States participation in World War I had been a great mistake. Their isolationist attitudes reflected convictions that American interests could not be harmed by developments abroad. Their disillusionment with Wilsonian idealism led them to minimize moral questions in foreign affairs. Their hatred of war drove them to try to prevent a recurrence of events which they believed had plunged the United States into war in 1917. In their revulsion against munitions makers and war profiteers, the revisionists wrote history that emphasized both economic motivation and self-interest.

As you read, consider these questions:

1   How did the Nye Committee reports stimulate writing along the revisionist line?

2 At the outbreak of war in Europe in 1914, President Wilson urged the American people to be neutral in thought as well as in deed. What evidence do you find in the Nye Committee reports that his admonition was followed by the people and by the United States government?

3 Several revisionist writers claimed that propaganda was responsible for American entry into World War I. Do you agree with what Grattan says in regard to the effects of propaganda? of economic pressures? Explain.

4 The revisionists denied that moral purposes were served by American intervention in World War I. Does the excerpt from Grattan bear out this attitude?

5 How does American determination to win trade and to acquire profits at the expense of strict neutrality provide a foundation for revisionist interpretation?

6 Why does disillusionment so frequently follow wars?

I

"THE MERCHANTS OF DEATH" AND WORLD WAR I

In April 1934 the United States Senate established the Senate Munitions Investigating Committee under the chairmanship of Senator Gerald P. Nye of North Dakota. The purpose of the committee was to examine thoroughly the munitions industry to discover the extent it influenced foreign policy. Coming at a time when the business community was under scrutiny by the New Deal administration, the investigation grew out of a popular concern about the activities of bankers and munitions manufacturers in relation to the war. The arms makers in particular became objects of such popular suspicion that the phrase "merchants of death" was widely used to describe them. The following excerpts are from summary reports on the findings of the Committee. ☐ 74th Congress, 2nd Session. Report No. 944, Part 3, pp. 1–4, 7–8. Washington, D.C.: U.S. Government Printing Office, 1936.

Earlier reports (74th Cong. Rept. 577) and a bill, H.R. 5529, as amended by the committee, represent the committee's contribution to the task of taking the profits out of war. This bill was unanimously recommended to Congress by the committee, and it is hoped that its early passage will serve as effective warning to all concerned that there will be no more profiteering in the unhappy eventuality that this Nation should again be engaged in war.

The committee has been in remarkable agreement on the need for neutrality legislation, following its studies of the adequacy of existing legislation upon which the Senate asked it to report. Its members have taken a most active part in securing the passage of new neutrality legislation, both in 1935 and in 1936, and believe that this legislation represents a great and wholesome advance in the interests of keeping this Nation out of foreign wars. . . .

I. THE NATURE OF THE MUNITIONS COMPANIES

The committee finds . . . that almost none of the munitions companies in this country confine themselves exclusively to the manufacture of military materials. . . . In addition to the manufacturers there are several sales companies which act as agents for various manufacturers. There are also brokers dealing largely in old and second-hand supplies. In case of war, other companies, not at present producing any munitions, would be called upon to furnish them. . . .

II. THE SALES METHODS OF THE MUNITIONS COMPANIES

The committee finds, under the head of sales methods of the munitions companies, that almost without exception, the American munitions companies investigated have at times resorted to such unusual approaches, questionable favors and commissions, and methods of "doing the needful" as to constitute, in effect, a form of bribery of foreign governmental officials or of their close friends in order to secure business.

The committee realizes that these were field practices by the agents of the companies, and were apparently in many cases part of a level of competition set by foreign companies, and that the heads of the American companies were, in cases, apparently unaware of their continued existence and shared the committee's distaste and disapprobation of such practices.

The committee accepts the evidence that the same practices are resorted to by European munitions companies, and that the whole process of selling arms abroad thus, in the words of a Colt agent, has "brought into play the most despicable side of human nature; lies, deceit, hypocrisy, greed, and graft occupying a most prominent part in the transactions."

The committee finds such practices on the part of any munitions company, domestic or foreign, to be highly unethical, a discredit to American business, and an unavoidable reflection upon those American governmental agencies which have unwittingly aided in the transactions . . . .

The committee finds, further, that the constant availability of munitions companies with competitive bribes ready in outstretched hands does not create a situation where the officials involved can, in the nature of things, be as much interested in peace and measures to secure peace as they are in increased armaments.

The committee finds also that there is a very considerable threat to the peace and civic progress of other nations in the success of the munitions makers and of their agents in corrupting the officials of any one nation and thereby selling to that one nation an armament out of proportion to its previous armaments. Whether such extraordinary sales are procured through bribery or through other forms of salesmanship, the effect of such sales is to produce fear, hostility, and greater munitions orders on the part of neighboring countries, culminating in economic strain and collapse or war.

The committee elsewhere takes note of the contempt of some of the munitions companies for those governmental departments and officials interested in securing peace, and finds here that continual or even occasional corruption of other governments naturally leads to a belief that all governments, including our own, must be controlled by economic forces entirely.

III. Their Activities Concerning Peace Efforts

The committee finds, under this head, that there is no record of any munitions company aiding any proposals for limitation of armaments, but that, on the contrary, there is a record of their active opposition by some to almost all such proposals, of resentment toward them, of contempt for those responsible for them, and of violation of such controls whenever established, and of rich profiting whenever such proposals failed. . . .

IV. The Effect of Armaments on Peace

The committee finds, under the head of the effect of armaments on peace, that some of the munitions companies have occasionally had opportunities to intensify the fears of people . . . to their own profit.

The committee finds, further, that the very quality which in civilian life tends to lead toward progressive civilization, namely the improvements of machinery, has been used by the munitions makers to scare nations into a continued frantic expenditure for the latest improvements in devices of warfare. The constant message of the traveling salesman of the munitions companies to the rest of the world has been that they now had available for sale something new, more dangerous and more deadly than ever before and that the potential enemy was or would be buying it.

While the evidence before this committee does not show that wars have been started solely because of the activities of munitions makers and their agents, it is also true that wars rarely have one single cause, and the committee finds it to be against the peace of the world for selfishly interested organizations to be left free to goad and frighten nations into military activity.

The committee finds, further, that munitions companies engaged in bribery find themselves involved in the civil and military politics of other nations, and that this is an unwarranted form of intrusion into the affairs of other nations and undesirable representation of the character and methods of the people of the United States.

By the end of 1934 the Nye Committee had shifted its emphasis from the munitions industry to an exposé of the influence of business interests on American intervention in World War I. □ 74th Congress, 2nd Session. Report Number 944, Part 6, pp. 2–3. Washington, D.C.: U.S. Government Printing Office, 1936.

The Committee finds that:

1. It is most important for the Nation and Congress to have full and exact information concerning all the changes in the neutrality policy made by the administration and the reasons for these changes. . . .

The Committee finds, according to testimony and exhibits introduced into the record . . . that in August 1914 the Department of State declared that loans by American banks to belligerent governments would be considered unneutral in spirit. This declaration had no legally binding power but the testimony indicates that if it had not been modified such loans would never have been made. The Committee is interested to observe that this ruling was made at a time when the American banks were reluctant to extend such loans. In October 1914 the Department, in a secret ruling officially revealed only to J. P. Morgan & Co. and the National City Bank of New York, made an artificial distinction between loans and credits, permitting the extension of the latter to belligerents. Although rumors of this change were published in the press at the time, no official statement was made until March 31, 1915. Meanwhile in an official letter of January 20, 1915, to the Chairman of the Senate Foreign Relations Committee, the Department failed to mention this distinction, thereby officially misinforming the Senate. The Committee is further of the opinion that this secret and artificial distinction permitted the beginning of the war trade and boom which later in 1915 produced a serious disbalance of American exports.

2. Loans to belligerents militate against neutrality, for when only one group of belligerents can purchase and transport commodities the loans act in

favor of that belligerent. They are especially unneutral when used to convert this country into an auxiliary arsenal for that belligerent who happens to control the seas, for that arsenal then becomes the subject of the military strategy of the other belligerent.

3. Such loans cannot but profoundly affect the neutrality of mind and spirit of those holding them. When the responsibility for the sale of such loans is placed by foreign belligerents in the hands of any one large banking group, as was done in the case of J. P. Morgan & Co. during the World War where out of some $2,500,000,000 allied indebtedness, J. P. Morgan & Co. arranged for or managed some $1,900,000,000, the concentrated power and influence of such loans on the neutrality of public opinion can be greatly accentuated. When the banking houses floating these loans are also financially interested in munitions companies depending for continued profits on foreign orders, the foreign belligerents have the power of securing the support of these banking houses for loans through favors to the munitions companies. . . .

4. Loans extended to the Allies in 1915 and 1916, led to a very considerable war boom and inflation. This boom extended beyond munitions to auxiliary supplies and equipment as well as to agricultural products. Such loans may be expected to produce a similar situation again. . . .

5. The nature of such a war-boom inflation is that, like all inflations, an administration is almost powerless to check it, once the movement is well started. Our foreign policy then is seriously affected by it, even to the extent of making impossible the alteration of our foreign policy in such a way as to protect our neutral rights.

6. The foreign policy of the United States from 1914 to 1917 was, in fact, affected by our growing trade with the Allies as well as by natural sympathies. The neutral rights we claimed were simply not enforced against our largest customers.

The Committee finds, on the basis of the testimony and exhibits introduced into the record and discussed in Chapter III, War Trade Expansion, that the development of the export of war commodities to the Allies resulted in a widespread expansion of almost all the lines of American business, an expansion which J. P. Morgan & Co., in their commercial agency contract, specifically undertook to stimulate. As a result by 1916 there was created a tremendous industrial machine, heavily capitalized, paying high wages, and dependent upon the purchasing power of the Allies. The Committee is of the opinion that this situation, with its risk of business depression and panic in event of damage to the belligerents' ability to purchase, involved the administration so inextricably it prevented the maintenance of a truly neutral course between the Allies and the Central Powers. Such a neutral course threatened to injure this export trade.

7. It is not desirable for the Nation that any foreign belligerent or any bankers representing them be allowed to get into a position as they did in 1915, when sudden stoppage of the support of sterling (or any other foreign exchange) can influence an administration into a reversal of our neutrality policy.

II

PROPAGANDA, TRADE, AND THE WAR

Through C. Hartley Grattan's book, from which the following reading was taken, runs the main themes of later revisionist writing. The volume stressed propaganda and economic motives for war, and it also censured President Wilson for his failure to resist pressures from economic and nationalistic groups. □ Reprinted by permission of the publisher, The Vanguard Press, from *Why We Fought* by C. Hartley Grattan, pp. 38–42, 71, 127, 135, 137–138, 140–141, 153, 155–156, 163–164. Copyright © 1929, 1957, by C. Hartley Grattan.

Modern war is fought on three fronts: the military, which includes the land, sea, and air forces; the economic, which includes all devices for weakening the enemy and strengthening the home front in this field; and the propagandistic. These fronts are not sharply distinct. The first is directed exclusively against the enemy, though it is of great use in overawing recalcitrant neutrals, while the latter are directed both against the enemy and against neutrals. Consequently we may assume that the United States was immediately subjected to economic and propagandistic pressure with a view of controlling its potentialities to the advantage of the group at work.

At this point we are interested in the propaganda. The leading student of the technique used in the [First] World War, Professor H. D. Lasswell, has isolated some general principles that were followed and which may be presumed to have controlled the propaganda agents in their work. The first principle was: "The war must not be due to a world system of conducting international affairs, nor to the stupidity or malevolence of all governing classes, but to the rapacity of the enemy." The war aims must be "idealistic" and "invidious at the expense of the enemy." A great deal must also be made of the "satanism" of the enemy. With these three principles to guide him an efficient propagandist could work with a reasonable hope of success. Above all, these positions had to be maintained with complete precision. Any blurring of the lines, any admissions of weakness, were not to be considered. It must be always a case of white vs. black, or good vs. evil.

BRITISH PROPAGANDA

An important condition of propaganda success is of course a favorable disposition amongst the people to be attacked. It is beyond question that the British propagandists, as has been remarked before, had little to do beyond confirming and elaborating prejudices already pretty firmly set in the American mind. . . .

. . . Amongst the American governing class, as constituted in 1914–1917, there was a distinct tradition of friendship for England. This was based on alleged cultural affinities, social alliances, commercial tie-ups and political agreements. . . .

. . . The American people were also favorably inclined toward England for her allegedly benevolent attitude during the Spanish-American War. The total effect was that, combined with the other factors enumerated, it was difficult for the British to imagine that there would be serious difficulties with America during the war. They, of course, were right.

It was not a time to take chances, however. The first step taken to control American opinion was to get control of all the cables between Europe and America. This not only gave the British control of the transmission of news—barring temporarily but not permanently the mails between neutrals in Europe and America and the wireless, which proved to be a relatively ineffective agent—but also of private communication between the United States and the belligerents. To do this required the cutting of but one cable, which was immediately done. . . .

Control of the cables is now recognized to be the most important cause for the astounding success the British had in manipulating the American mind, quite apart from the favorable disposition of the American people. It is emphasized by every writer who touches on the subject. Mr. Bertrand Russell wrote: ". . . Allied propaganda, through British control of the cables, secured wider publicity than that of Germany, and achieved a notable success in winning the sympathy and ultimately the cooperation of the United States." . . .

It would be possible to . . . discuss endless atrocity yarns in details, showing by example wherein each story was either false, or the angle of attack was deliberately perverted to make a case against Germany. The British propagandists counted heavily on the naiveté of the civil populations of all countries and of the American public in particular. It can hardly be said that their confidence was misplaced. "The sound sense of the masses," Georg Brandes [a Danish literary critic] wrote, "and their intuitive conception of right have never been anything but a democratic legend. For the masses believe, as a rule, every lie that is cleverly presented to them."

ECONOMICS

Economics provides the dynamics of history. No reasonable account of an historical event can be written without a careful consideration of the economic forces of which it is the expression. Yet it is beyond question that there is no absolute stimulus-response relation between economic facts and political conduct. To accept such a position is to ignore the capacity of mankind to rationalize its conduct in ways more flattering to its self-esteem than a frank admission that dollars and goods rule. Economics provides the ground to walk on, while the rationalizations give the excuse for walking.

The [First] World War is on all fours with every other war in having an economic foundation. Every reputable historian who has dealt with it, no matter how great his preoccupation with the diplomacy of its precipitation, regards the diplomacy, the propaganda, the alleged aims and objects for fighting, as mere secondary structures reared on the foundation of money and trade. The flag follows trade, the politicians follow the flag, the propagandists follow the politicians, and the people follow the propagandists. . . .

. . . Our trade with Germany before the war was almost as large as that of the British Empire: the Empire provided 18.2 per cent of the German imports, while the United States provided 15.9 per cent. The United States stood second on the German import list. The British trade was sacrificed to the war, while the American was sacrificed to the British blockade.

Most striking is the decided increase of trade [during the war] between the United States and the Allied powers. Our exports to the United Kingdom increased from approximately one-quarter of our total trade to approximately one-third. At the same time our imports from the same source declined from approximately one-sixth to approximately one-eighth. With France, American exports changed from a little over one-twentieth of the total to nearly one-sixth. Our imports from France declined from a little less than one-twelfth of the total to less than one-twentieth. This occurred at the same time that our exports to Germany declined from a little more than one-eighth of the total to less than one-hundredth; and while our imports from Germany declined from approximately one-tenth of the total to less than one-hundredth. In other words our economic ties with the Allies increased with astounding rapidity while at the same time our economic ties with Germany all but disappeared. That this should be without effect on American sentiment is simply a position that cannot be maintained.

The munitions trade, as has been remarked, caused more excitement than all the rest of the war supplies trade. This was due, no doubt, to the obvious fact that munitions were used in the killing of the enemy, and aroused the humanitarian feelings of the Americans . . . . The argument ran that since Germany was cut off from America by the British blockade, the American Government should prohibit the shipment of munitions to the Allies and so make the situation more equitable. Another line of argument was that since the Allies were obstinate about meeting our demands that they observe American neutral rights under international law, an embargo be placed on munitions (sometimes on war supplies generally), until such time as they would listen to reason. The agitation never succeeded in getting the munitions trade restricted in any way whatsoever. The heaviest burden it had to bear was a sizable excise tax. . . .

The shipment of munitions to the Allies did as much to embitter relations between Germany and the United States as any other cause. It seems beyond question that nothing went so far to convince the German public, as well as the official class, that the United States was hostile to Germany as the official position the State Department maintained toward the traffic. The munitions affair was second only to the American attitude toward the British blockade in convincing the German public that it had nothing to expect from America in the way of relief from the intolerable pressure exerted upon her by the Allies. Ambassador Gerard has written: ". . . I have spoken of the subject of the selling of arms and supplies by America to the Allies. No German ever forgets this. The question of legality or treaties never enters his mind: he only knows that American supplies and munitions killed his brother, son or father." The Germans began to feel bitter toward America even before Americans began to feel bitter toward Germany. . . .

A cursory examination of the relevant material will show that the controversy rose slowly and became violent in proportion as we supplied the Allies with munitions. It originated in 1914, increased in bitterness in 1915, and came to a climax in 1916, to be continued by the bitter-enders through 1916 right up to the entrance of America into the war. However, the futility of hoping that anything would be done about it by the American Government was clearly apparent in early 1916, though for a moment in September, the agitators were given reason to hope for action, as we shall see in another connection. The controversy need not be traced here beyond the spring of 1916. We shall see that when it was necessary to put pressure on the Allies it was easier to strike at them through the field of finance. There was never much possibility that an embargo on munitions would be laid, though the idea did receive the sympathetic consideration of American Government officials including President Wilson. . . .

Purchasing [of war materials] on such an enormous scale required equally extensive financing, a problem to which J. P. Morgan and Company also addressed itself. The procedures followed were, (a) the shipment of gold from London to New York, (b) the selling of American securities formerly held abroad, and (c) the placing of loans in America. This movement transformed America from a debtor to a creditor nation. . . .

Nevertheless, none of these devices—gold shipments and security sales—could meet the demand for money. It has been estimated that the war was financed on borrowed money to the extent of 65 per cent. It was the loans to the Allied powers, which were almost entirely spent in America, that did more than anything else to tie American finance to the Allied cause. . . .

From figures cited earlier in this section it appears that our foreign trade in wartime was concentrated to the extent of 50 per cent with France and England. What proportion of this was strictly confined to munitions and war material and other contraband is not of importance to the present argument. The point here is that approximately 50 per cent of our foreign trade had to pass through the war zone to belligerent powers. It was, therefore, subjected to risk from German submarines—for the submarine, as the campaign was conducted in unrestricted fashion, did not discriminate between contraband and non-contraband. We have also seen that in 1915 and 1916, approximately 85 per cent of this trade was carried in foreign-owned bottoms [or ships]. Let us assume that of this figure the proportion of 70 per cent was carried in bottoms belonging to the enemies of Germany. It was to Germany's interest to sink the vessels of her enemies. It was to America's economic interest that nothing be placed in the way of landing her goods in Allied countries. When the two interests clashed, we followed the direction of our economic interest. We tried to prevent the Germans using their submarines.

PROBLEM 12

The Submarine Issue

The critical importance of President Wilson's role in the American intervention of 1917 is recognized by nearly all students of the period. The revisionists criticized the President severely on a number of grounds. They blamed him for failing to insist on British observance of the Declaration of London, a statement of neutral rights adopted by an international conference in 1909 but never ratified by Britain. They charged him with reversing himself in allowing private loans to the belligerents, and they objected to his opposition to the Gore-McLemore resolutions which would have forbidden Americans to travel on belligerent ships in the war zones. His refusal to advocate an arms embargo was laid to the influence of business on him.

Charles Seymour, who has been called the dean of American writers on this subject, presented a different point of view in two books, *American Diplomacy During the World War* (1934) and *American Neutrality, 1914–1917* (1935). Seymour had also edited the *Intimate Papers of Colonel House* (in four volumes, published from 1926 to 1928), which followed the idealistic interpretation. His books of the mid-1930's carefully analyzed Wilson's diplomatic record. They showed some recognition of the weight of revisionist charges, but insisted on the importance of the essentially moral character of

Wilson's motives. Wilson saw the submarine threat as a moral challenge because of its ruthless disregard for human life. He tried to maintain a neutral policy and there were times when United States relations with England were more strained than were its relations with Germany. Wilson had two objectives: to preserve the peace and to protect American rights. In the end he was unable to reconcile these two aims.

The Seymour reading in Problem 12 raises the question of how important is a single element in a complex situation. By isolating one factor—submarine warfare—without which, Seymour believed, the United States would not have intervened, he argued for the overriding importance of a single cause.

As you read, consider these questions:

1   Does Seymour weaken his case when he admits the strong economic pressures on President Wilson? Explain.

2   The Germans announced a policy of unrestricted submarine warfare in 1917. If you were a high-ranking German official in 1917, would you have favored the policy of unrestricted submarine warfare?

3   Other neutral nations did not take an uncompromising attitude with regard to German submarine warfare. Why then did the United States take such an attitude? What else might Wilson have done?

4   "War causation is never found in a single issue. To isolate a single cause is to oversimplify the complexities of history." After reading the excerpt from Seymour, do you agree with this point of view?

THE ESSENTIAL CAUSE OF THE WAR

Charles Seymour's purpose was to revise the revisionists. Believing the attack on President Wilson to be unfair, he examined Wilson's motives objectively, using original documentary sources as a basis for his conclusions. By limiting the problem of what caused the war to issues of neutral rights between 1914 and 1917, he produced a strong case for the argument that the submarine campaign led to American participation in the war. □ Charles Seymour, *American Neutrality, 1914-1917*, pp. 1-11, 168-171. New Haven: Yale University Press. Copyright © 1935.

Recent discussions [in 1935] of the causes of American intervention in the [First] World War have stirred emotions; but they have failed to suggest conclusively measures that might have served to keep us at peace. There is talk of the intrigues of munitions makers and the greed of capitalists. Less fantastic is the revival of the thesis that if we had treated Germany and the Allies with an even hand in meeting their attacks upon American neutral rights, we might have avoided intervention. A popular outline of the years

1914–17, by Mr. Walter Millis, implies that as we had permitted infractions of our rights by the Allies we had no right to protest to the point of war against Germany's use of the submarine. But he suggests no practicable alternatives to the policy followed by President Wilson. The country slithered into war, he evidently feels, much as Lloyd George once remarked that Europe had slithered into war in 1914. "Among them all," Mr. Millis writes of the Americans of 1917, "none quite knew how it had happened, nor why. . . ."

There was at least one American who was acutely aware of why the United States was brought into the World War. This was the President of the United States, who for nearly three years struggled to maintain neutrality in the face of difficulties that finally proved uncontrollable. Whether as a basis for future policy, or merely to set the historical record straight, it is worth while to review Woodrow Wilson's fight to avoid intervention.

Any inquiry into the causes of American participation in the war must begin with the personality of Wilson. His office conferred upon him a determining influence in foreign policy which was heightened by the troubled state of affairs abroad. His character was such that he never let this influence slip into other hands. He was his own foreign secretary. Conscious of the power and character of public opinion, "under bonds," as he put it, to public sentiment, he nevertheless made the major decisions on his own responsibility. He delivered his "too proud to fight" speech and he sent [Johann von] Bernstorff [the German ambassador] home without stopping to ask what the man in the street would say. Dominant sentiment in the United States was certainly pro-Ally. American economic prosperity, furthermore, depended upon the maintenance of our trade with the Allies. But it is a far cry from these facts to the assumption that because of them we adopted a policy that pointed toward intervention. It would be necessary to show that emotional sympathy and material interests overcame the strong pacifistic sentiment of Congress and people. It would especially be necessary to show that because of them Wilson first adopted a discriminatory attitude toward Germany and then surrendered his determination to keep the country out of war.

Ample evidence is now available regarding Wilson's sentiments toward the belligerents. If it reveals an underlying personal sympathy with the Allies, it also reveals a studied insistence not to permit that feeling to affect national policy. He was so far successful that he was attacked in turn by each belligerent group as being favorable to the other. There can be no question that he regarded the maintenance of peace as his first duty. Always he held to the double principle he formulated at the moment he was smarting under the news of the *Arabic's* sinking in August, 1915: "1. The people of this country count on me to keep them out of the war; 2. It would be a calamity to the world at large if we should be actively drawn into the conflict and so deprived of all disinterested influence over the settlement." He maintained this attitude in the face of what he regarded as gross affronts by Germany. "The country is undoubtedly back of me in the whole matter," he wrote privately in September, 1915, "and I feel myself under bonds to it to show patience to the utmost. My chief puzzle is to determine where patience ceases to be a virtue."

But across the determination to preserve peace ran the equally strong determination to preserve the neutral rights of the country. There was a higher principle which the President placed above peace: the honor of the United States. The outcome of this contradiction would be determined not by Wilson's policy but by that of the belligerents. He said in January, 1916:

"I know that you are depending upon me to keep this Nation out of the war. So far I have done so and I pledge you my word that, God helping me, I will—if it is possible. But you have laid another duty upon me. You have bidden me to see to it that nothing stains or impairs the honor of the United States, and that is a matter not within my control; that depends upon what others do, not upon what the Government of the United States does. Therefore there may at any moment come a time when I cannot preserve both the honor and the peace of the United States. Do not exact of me an impossible and contradictory thing."

Against both groups of belligerents Wilson steadily maintained American neutral rights. It is by no means a fact that he accepted British and Allied infractions of what he described as "hitherto fixed international law." The notes of protest which he sponsored and which so greatly annoyed those who, like Ambassador [to Great Britain Walter Hines] Page, frankly favored the Allied cause, made clear that the United States did not, and would not, recognize the legality of the Allied pseudo-blockade. In the late summer of 1916 the President secured from Congress wide powers permitting him to prohibit loans and to impose embargoes if retaliatory measures appeared advisable. A few weeks later he asked [his adviser Colonel Edward M.] House to warn Sir Edward Grey [the British foreign secretary] "in the strongest terms" that the American people were "growing more and more impatient with the intolerable conditions of neutrality, their feeling as hot against Great Britain as it was first against Germany. . . . "

That he did not actually exercise the pressure of embargoes against the British and French resulted from two factors. The first was that the conflict over Allied interference with neutral trade was pushed into the background at critical moments by the more immediate and intense conflict with Germany over the submarine campaign. "If Germany had not alienated American sympathies," wrote Colonel House, "by her mode of warfare, the United States would not have put up with Allied control of American trade on the high seas." The fact has been emphasized by Winston Churchill: "The first German U-boat campaign," he writes, "gave us our greatest assistance. It altered the whole position of our controversies with America. A great relief became immediately apparent."

The second reason for not pushing the diplomatic conflict with the Allies to the point of retaliatory measures lay in the economic interests of America. Any practicable measures designed to enforce our interpretation of international law would have ruined the interests they meant to safeguard. By our formal protests we protected our ultimate property rights and built up a case for future damages to be proved before an international tribunal. Through private negotiations we secured in large measure the protection of immediate commercial interests. Whatever the inconvenience and delays experienced in our trade with the northern European neutrals, American foreign commerce was deriving rich profits. Allied command of the sea did not touch our pockets so much as our pride. As Ambassador Spring Rice cabled to Grey, it seemed "Objectionable not because it is what it is, but because it is so all-pervading." Thus, if Wilson had destroyed the basis of our prosperity in order to compel immediate acceptance of the American interpretation of international law, which very few Americans understood and which even now is not entirely clear, he would have provoked something like a revolt against his administration. "If it came to the last analysis," wrote House to Wilson in the summer of 1915, "and we placed an embargo upon munitions of war and foodstuffs to please the cotton men, our whole industrial and agricultural machinery would cry out against it." Wilson's policy was designed not to favor the Allies but to protect the immediate interests of the nation and at the same time to preserve our ultimate legal rights. He yielded no principle and surrendered no claim.

The German attack upon American rights Wilson believed to be of an entirely different nature and one that must be met by different methods. The intensive submarine campaign was the answer to the system of Allied maritime control; logically, an excuse might be found for it. But its effects upon neutral rights were far more disastrous. For technical reasons and to operate effectively, the submarines must make their attack without warning, destroy blindly, escape as speedily as possible, leaving the sinking merchant ship, which might be neutral or belligerent, which might or might not carry contraband, with no assurance of what would happen to passengers and crew.

To Wilson and to dominant American opinion, such wholesale methods of destroying enemy and neutral commerce were shocking.This was no question of "juridical niceties." The submarine campaign, unlike the Allied blockade, involved undiscriminating destruction of American property rights. It permitted no distinction between contraband and free goods. The Allied system gave to the American shipper reasonable assurance of safe passage after he had complied with certain formalities. Under the threat of the submarine the shipper faced the risk of losing his entire cargo. The Allied system did not involve the loss of American ships; if held in a British prize court the owner could find protection for them in legal procedure. The German submarine threatened the loss of the ship and the death of crew and passengers as well.

Thus, from the point of view of material interests, there could be no comparison between the damage resulting to Americans from the Allied blockade and that from the intensive submarine campaign. If the latter were permitted, under protests comparable to those sent to the Allies, the result would be an almost complete blockade of American commerce, since shippers would not dare send cargoes and crew out to destruction. A clear illustration of the effect of the submarine campaign on American commercial, industrial, and agricultural interests was given by the congestion of our ports that followed the threat of submarine attacks in February and March, 1917. Freights were snarled, goods were spoiled, business was menaced with a complete tie-up.

Even so, Wilson might not have taken his firm stand against the submarine if merely property rights had been threatened. He was always careful not to interpret national policy in terms of purely material interests. Despite the difficulties involved, the economic aspects of the diplomatic conflict with Germany might have been adjudicated. But the submarine warfare involved attacks upon American lives, whether sailors on merchant ships or passengers.

To Wilson it seemed a war on humanity. Between property interests and human rights there lay a clear distinction. It was brought home to all America when, on May 7, 1915, the *Lusitania* was sunk without warning, over eleven hundred persons drowned, men, women, and children, among them more than one hundred and twenty Americans. . . .

The principle of utilizing history as a guide to policy is entirely sound, but care must be taken to see that deductions from the past are valid. Easy generalizations are worse than useless. It may well be that we can learn much from our experience of the years 1914–17 that will help us to stay out of future European wars; but we must be chary of assuming that conditions in the future will be at all similar to those of the past. We must be especially suspicious of any simple solution to the problem of neutrality, which by its nature is essentially complex.

It is obviously of importance that we clear the decks by discarding various prevalent impressions of what took us into the last war. Thus it is quite inexact to state that we were drawn in by our export of munitions, which forced the Germans to adopt the method of ruthless submarine warfare. As we have seen, all the evidence available goes to show that even without American export of munitions to the Allies the Germans would have utilized the unrestricted submarine campaign, as the only effective means of striking at Great Britain, which was regarded as the backbone of the Entente Alliance. It is even further from the truth to state that our inter-intervention was determined by pressure from financial groups which had acquired a vast stake in the fortunes of the Allies. Whatever the size of that stake it was largely secured, regardless of Allied victory; it was by no means concentrated in the hands of bankers, but distributed throughout the widely spread groups in America which were strongly pacific. If businessmen or bankers might be supposed to have had an interest in American participation in the war, they had no means of exercising pressure upon the President or upon Congress. We know as a historical fact that no effective pressure was exercised.

Another explanation of our entrance into the war, not so popular for it is not so simple, implies that because of the importance of our war trade with the Allies we put ourselves in a position where we could not exercise effective pressure against them, in the defense of our interests; and that we entered virtually into an economic, if not a political, alliance with them.

The argument continues, that Germany could thus justifiably take any measures against that economic alliance, even if such measures injured our neutral rights, and that we merely got what we might have expected. Such a position has elements of far greater apparent historical strength. But it is misleading in that it ignores the point, so frequently made by the German Ambassador, that by injecting the submarine issue at recurringly critical moments from 1915 on, Germany herself made it difficult or impossible for America to meet Allied infractions of commercial rights.

Except for the submarine, our quarrel would have been with the Allies. Upon this Bernstorff, Grey, and [Robert] Lansing [Secretary of State] are agreed. In such a case, it is entirely improbable that the diplomatic dispute would have developed into war. Sentimental considerations, economic interests, sympathies of political leaders, all would have combined to produce a peaceful settlement of the quarrel. But all those factors, on the other hand, would have been powerless to drive us into war with Germany if it had not been for the German submarine campaign. There lay the positive cause of American intervention. It is historically isolated, as one isolates a microbe. This can be asserted with confidence, since it is the one cause which if removed would have left us at peace. Without the submarine campaign, we should not have entered the war, whatever other circumstances were operative.

PROBLEM 13

Intervention
for American Security

During World War I, some of President Wilson's closest advisers believed that the safety of the nation was the most vital issue. Walter Hines Page and Colonel Edward M. House regarded the war as a contest between democracy and German militarism, but they saw it also as a fight for the preservation of the American democratic system. Secretary of State Robert Lansing was probably more deeply concerned over the quest for security than any of Wilson's advisers. In 1917 these influential Americans and many others believed that if Germany triumphed over Great Britain and France, it would then turn on the United States.

In 1943 Walter Lippmann, the well-known journalist and publicist, wrote a persuasive book, *U.S. Foreign Policy: Shield of the Republic.* In it he argued that the American people supported Wilson because they "recognized intuitively" the German menace to their security.

Writing some years later, other "realists," like Hans Morgenthau, Robert E. Osgood, and George F. Kennan, doubted that Americans generally were conscious of the dangers of 1917, but these writers, no less than Lippmann, stressed self-interest and national safety. Kennan argued that although some Americans understood the issues at stake, the national mind was too emotional to comprehend the real foundations of American security. The ideas of these writers were shaped somewhat by the circumstances of their own times. Watching nations seek great power to satisfy selfish interests, the "realists" were skeptical of the utility of moralism in foreign policy and viewed it as mere sentimentality. They argued that national security depended on a balance of power among the great nations of the world. Their rejection of Wilsonian idealism did not mean, however, that they would deny the importance of democratic principles.

The readings in Problem 13 by Walter Lippmann and George F. Kennan consider the problem of American entry from the broad perspective of developments since 1900. From a mid-twentieth-century background of increasing world tensions and difficulties, these authors view American intervention in World War I. As you read, consider these questions:

1 Lippmann states that Theodore Roosevelt had "the elements of a genuine foreign policy," while Woodrow Wilson's administration lacked "even the rudiments of a settled foreign policy." How well does the first selection support these statements?

2 Lippmann argues that President Wilson had chosen "superficial reasons" for declaring war, but because a majority of the people realized what a German victory would mean, they supported the President. Does this interpretation mean that President Wilson asked for American entry into the war for one reason and that the American public agreed for another?

3 What essential difference—if any—do you see in the views of Lippmann and Kennan?

4 In the selection by Kennan, do you feel that it is his primary concern to explain why America entered World War I? What seems to be at the root of his motives in this essay on American diplomacy?

5 Does Kennan suggest how democracy can become more effective in preventing war? Can democracy in foreign policy help promote world peace?

I

AN UNCONSCIOUS QUEST FOR SECURITY

During the period between the two world wars, Walter Lippmann was one of the most widely read and influential political commentators. In the book from which the following excerpt is taken, he maintained that while the submarine provided the occasion for going to war, the real reason was the German threat to the Atlantic community. The crime committed by Germany, as Lippman saw it, was that Germany tried to destroy the highways by which the Atlantic powers lived. Lippmann made these same points in an editorial in the *New Republic* for February 17, 1917. ☐ From *U.S. Foreign Policy: Shield of the Republic,* by Walter Lippmann, pp. 25–26, 27, 28–39, by permission of Little, Brown and Company—Atlantic Monthly Press. Copyright © 1943 by Walter Lippmann.

The turn of the century was a critical period in the history of the Republic. For by that time the foreign commitments of the United States, which could be validated in the last analysis only by successful war, had been extended over an immense section of the surface of the globe. On the Atlantic side the line ran approximately from Greenland to the shoulder of Brazil, at about 35° west longitude. On the Pacific side the line was at about 120° east longitude in the Philippines, and even beyond, as the events of 1941 showed, in so far as we were committed to oppose the dismemberment of China. The direct American commitment included the defense of territory from Alaska to Luzon, from Greenland to Brazil, from Canada to the Argentine.

This immense commitment had been made, to be exact, by February 1899. It had been made eighteen years before the United States entered the first World War and some forty-two years before the Japanese attack on Pearl Harbor. No further military commitment of any consequence was made by the United States during the twentieth century. All American military commitments had been made by the end of the nineteenth century. The history of our foreign relations in the twentieth century is a story of failure. It is the story of our national failure to balance the commitments which were made in the nineteenth century. Because of that failure we have been compelled to fight two great unexpected wars for which we were unprepared.

The period of unending domestic controversy over American foreign relations began in January 1899 when the Treaty of Paris, which concluded the war with Spain, was submitted to the Senate for ratification. . . .

The wisdom of the immense commitment to superimpose upon the Monroe Doctrine what [Captain Alfred Thayer] Mahan [a writer of naval history] called "Asiatic dominion" was hotly debated not only in the Senate, but in the McKinley-Bryan elections of 1900. It is too late to debate it now. What cannot be gainsaid, however, is that the subsequent foreign policy of the United States has never been equal to the size of the commitment. From the day when Admiral [George] Dewey sailed into Manila Bay until the day when General [Jonathan M.] Wainwright surrendered Corregidor, the United States never made a sustained and prudent, or remotely adequate, effort to bring its obligations and its power into balance.

President Theodore Roosevelt, who, with Senator [Henry Cabot] Lodge and Captain Mahan, was the principle promoter of the commitment, did realize that the new departure called for new measures. He saw that we had assumed vast responsibilities in the two oceans. So he insisted upon digging the Panama Canal in order that the navy could be concentrated rapidly in either ocean. He persuaded Congress and the people to support the construction of an enlarged and modern navy.

In his own mind he went further, though he never explained it to the nation or made it a matter of avowed national policy. He knew that in 1900 Germany had staked out her claim to world power by deciding to build a navy so large that it compelled Great Britain "to set about the reduction of her outlying squadrons with a view to mustering her full strength in home waters." He knew that Germany was jealous of the American annexation of the Philippines, and had ordered Admiral von Diederichs to Manila to watch Admiral Dewey. He knew that two days before the battle of Manila Bay, John Hay had sent a telegram from London saying of Germany, *"Voilà l'ennemi* in the present crisis."

Theodore Roosevelt realized that to support our commitments we needed not only the Panama Canal and a strong navy, but also friends and virtual allies—allies against the rising imperialism of Germany, and later on against the rising imperialism of Japan. For that reason President Roosevelt and his Secretary of State, John Hay, never allowed disputes about financial concessions in China to alienate the United States from Great Britain. For the same reason he [President Roosevelt] intervened quickly in the Moroccan Affair of 1905 in order to prevent a European war which, he realized, would leave the United States alone with its vast commitments.

Theodore Roosevelt had, therefore, the elements of a genuine foreign policy. Aware of the American commitments, he sought to develop—though tentatively, unsurely, and without making the matter plain to the nation—the elements of American power: our strategic position by constructing the Panama Canal, our armaments by enlarging the navy, our alliances by adhering to those powers who were our friends and the opponents of our opponents. But these rudimentary beginnings of a true foreign policy were not carried forward by Theodore Roosevelt's successors. . . .

. . . The mental habits of Theodore Roosevelt's immediate successors—Taft and Wilson—were formed in that period of illusory isolation which had lasted from 1823 to 1898. Both were idealists who habitually rejected the premises of the politics of power. Both disliked armaments. In them the idealism which prompts Americans to make large and resounding commitments was combined with the pacifism which causes Americans to shrink from the measures of force that are needed to support the commitments. Neither prompted the preparation of armaments in time of peace. Both accepted reluctantly and tardily the need to arm. Both abhorred as inherently vicious and unnecessary, and as contrary to American principles, the formation of alliances. But both favored a League of Nations in which the United States assumed the obligation to enforce peace.

Thus the seeds of a genuine foreign policy, which Theodore Roosevelt planted, never matured. A national understanding of what is a foreign policy was never inculcated into the minds of the later American generations. When the long-expected war in Europe broke out in 1914, the United States had no foreign policy which enabled the nation to determine its interests in the conflict. President Wilson had no foreign policy, accepted by the nation, which gave him the means of judging whether, why, when, where, how, and to what end, the United States must take its position in the war.

From 1914 to 1916 Wilson vacillated between the assertion of American rights and reluctance to face the consequences of asserting them, between dread of a German victory and dread of a war to prevent a German victory. Thus he took a zigzag course, now one way because the British blockade infringed the American doctrine of the freedom of the seas, now the other way because German ruthlessness outraged American sensibilities. Lacking a foreign policy, and with leaders whose training was wholly in domestic politics, the nation had no means of ascertaining its true interests. The verbal battle of the propagandists, of which so much was made in later years, was fought in this vacuum of the American mind. It was fought because the American nation lacked even the rudiments of a settled foreign policy which could make clear whose victory and what kind of victory would best serve the vital interests of the United States.

Because of this vacuum, the United States went to war in April 1917 for reasons which were never willingly or accurately avowed. And so they were never clearly recognized.

The occasion for going to war was Germany's unrestricted use of the submarine against American merchant shipping on the Atlantic routes from North America to the British Isles and France. But the substantial and compelling reason for going to war was that the cutting of the Atlantic communications meant the starvation of Britain and, therefore, the conquest of Western Europe by imperial Germany.

President Wilson avoided this explanation of his decision to intervene, choosing instead to base his decision upon the specific legal objection to unrestricted submarine warfare and upon a generalized moral objection to lawless and cruel aggression. But these superficial reasons for the declaration of war would never have carried the day if a majority of the people had not recognized intuitively, and if some Americans had not seen clearly, what the threatened German victory would mean to the United States. Though there was lacking the tradition of a foreign policy which made the matter self-evident, many Americans saw in 1917 that if Germany won, the United States would have to face a new and aggressively expanding German empire which had made Britain, France, and Russia its vassals, and Japan its ally. They saw that in such a position the defense of the Western Hemisphere would require immense armaments over and above those needed in the Pacific, and that America would have to live in a perpetual state of high and alert military preparedness. It was in this very concrete and practical sense, though un-happily President Wilson preferred not to particularize, that a German victory in 1917 would have made the world unsafe for the American democracies from Canada to the Argentine.

This in brief was the undeclared, and only partially realized, foreign policy which determined the participation of the United States in the first German World War. The sinking of merchant ships without visit and search, and without provision for the safety of crews and passengers, would not in itself have been the *casus belli* if the German submarines had caused less destruction. Sporadic sinkings would have continued to lead to protests, as they did in 1915 and 1916, and probably to reprisals. But they would not have led to war if by 1917 the submarine had not become so destructive as to make it seem probable that Germany would starve out Britain and isolate France.

Nor did the United States go to war to make the world safe for all democracies: if it had seemed probable that Germany would be defeated by Czarist Russia, the United States would have remained neutral because its vital interests in the North Atlantic would have remained secure. The war was certainly not engaged to overthrow the Kaiser and to make Germany a democratic republic: if the Germans had not broken into the Atlantic and threatened the whole structure of our Atlantic defenses, private citizens would still have made faces at the Kaiser, but the nation would not have made war upon him.

The United States did not go to war because it wished to found a League of Nations; it went to war in order to preserve American security. And when the war was over, the nation would almost certainly have accepted in some form or other the scheme of the League of Nations if President Wilson had been able to demonstrate to the people that the League would perpetuate the security which the military victory had won for them. Mr. Wilson failed to make this demonstration. He failed because in leading the nation to war he had failed to give the durable and compelling reasons for the momentous decision. The reasons he did give were legalistic and moralistic and idealistic reasons, rather than the substantial and vital reason that the security of the United States demanded that no aggressively expanding imperial power, like Germany, should be allowed to gain the mastery of the Atlantic Ocean.

Because this simple and self-evident American interest was not candidly made explicit, the nation never understood clearly why it had entered the war. As time went on, the country was, therefore, open to every suggestion and insinuation that the nation had fought for no good reason at all, that its victory was meaningless, that it had been maneuvered into a non-American war by the international bankers and the British diplomats. And so, having failed to make plain that the war was waged for a vital American interest, President Wilson had no way of proving to the nation that his settlement of the war really concerned the United States. The war had been fought without a foreign policy, and neither President Wilson nor the nation had the means, therefore, of judging whether the League was merely a foreign or was also an American interest. . . .

Not until twenty years later, not until France had fallen and Britain was in mortal peril, not until the Japanese had surrounded the Philippines, did it become possible for the nation to perceive the hidden but real structure of America's strategic position in the world.

II

THE PRICE OF INDIFFERENCE

In the book from which the following excerpt was taken, George F. Kennan, a career diplomat and historian, pointed out that the security of the United States in 1917 lay in the delicate balance of power in Europe. The idealism, he claimed, which impelled Americans to fight the war to the bitter end, also helped destroy the balance which had preserved peace in Europe for a century. Kennan was an influential member of the policy planning staff of the State Department which devised the Marshall Plan. □ Reprinted from *American Diplomacy, 1900–1950,* by George F. Kennan by permission of The University of Chicago Press. Copyright © 1951 by The University of Chicago.

I would not want it thought that anything I am about to say indicates any lack of sympathy for Woodrow Wilson or of appreciation for the depth and bitterness of his problems. But none of this absolves us from the duty of looking coldly and critically at the nature of our national reaction to such a challenge.

In the first place, with respect to the origins of the war: let us note that there was for long no understanding in this country that either the origins or the issues of the war were of any concern to us. Speaking in 1916, President Wilson said that with the objects and causes of the war "we are not concerned. The obscure foundations from which its stupendous flood has burst forth we are not interested to search for or explore." "America," he said on a later occasion, "did not at first see the full meaning of the war. It looked like a natural raking out of the pent-up jealousies and rivalries of the complicated politics of Europe." Here, we may note, there was no recognition that what might be at issue in the European war was anything that concerned us. . . .

Proceeding on this basis, it was logical that the only American interest in the war we were inclined to recognize for a long time was the defense of our neutral rights according to the established laws of maritime warfare, as they had been known in the past. We did not understand that new modalities of warfare and new weapons—above all, the total blockade and the submarine—had rendered obsolete some of the more important of these rules. Not only had their observance become physically impracticable, but each side had come to feel that its chances of victory and survival depended on the violation of one or another of them. Either side would have preferred to accept war with us rather than refrain from violating certain ones of them. This meant that a strict insistence by us on their observance could eventually lead us, theoretically, into war with both belligerents—a paradoxical ending for a policy designed to keep us out of war.

Looking backward today on these endless disputes between our government and the belligerents over neutral rights, it seems hard to understand how we could have attached so much importance to them. They irritated both belligerents and burdened our relations with them, and I find it hard to believe that they involved our national honor. It might be our privilege to defend the rights of our citizens to travel on belligerent vessels, but it was hardly a duty, unless we chose to define it as a duty to ourselves.

As time went on, there grew up, of course, alongside this outlook, something quite different: a realization of the danger of defeat that confronted the Entente powers and an awareness of the damage that would be done to our world position by the elimination of England as a strong force in the world. In addition to this, the superiority of British propaganda, and other factors, began to work to the benefit of the Allied cause. The result was a gradual growth of pro-Allied sentiment, and particularly in the minds of the responsible American leaders. This sentiment was enough to cause [President] Wilson and [Colonel Edward M.] House to water down our neutrality policy to the benefit of the British and to make cautious efforts to stop the war, in 1915 and 1916, as the best means of averting the danger of a British defeat. But this pro-Ally feeling was never sufficient to constitute, for the national consciousness as a whole, adequate justification for entering the war; and you will remember that our entry, when it came, was over an issue of neutrality.

Once in the war, we had no difficulty in discovering—and lost no time in doing so—that the issues involved in it were of the greatest significance to us.

It is surely a curious characteristic of democracy; this amazing ability to shift gears overnight in one's ideological attitudes, depending on whether one considers one's self at war or at peace. Day before yesterday, let us say, the issues at stake between ourselves and another power were not worth the life of a single American boy. Today, nothing else counts at all; our cause is holy; the cost is no consideration; violence must know no limitations short of unconditional surrender.

Now I know the answer to this one. A democracy is peace-loving. It does not like to go to war. It is slow to rise to provocation. When it has once been provoked to the point where it must grasp the sword, it does not easily forgive its adversary for having produced this situation. The fact of the provocation then becomes itself the issue. Democracy fights in anger—it fights for the very reason that it was forced to go to war. It fights to punish the power that was rash enough and hostile enough to provoke it—to teach that power a lesson it will not forget, to prevent the thing from happening again. Such a war must be carried to the bitter end.

This is true enough, and, if nations could afford to operate in the moral climate of individual ethics, it would be understandable and acceptable. But I sometimes wonder whether in this respect a democracy is not uncomfortably similar to one of those prehistoric monsters with a body as long as this room and a brain the size of a pin: he lies there in his comfortable primeval mud and pays little attention to his environment; he is slow to wrath—in fact, you practically have to whack his tail off to make him aware that his interests are being disturbed; but, once he grasps this, he lays about him with such blind determination that he not only destroys his adversary but largely wrecks his native habitat. You wonder whether it would not have been wiser for him to have taken a little more interest in what was going on at an earlier date and to have seen whether he could not have prevented some of these situations from arising instead of proceeding from an undiscriminating indifference to a holy wrath equally undiscriminating.

In any case, once we were at war, it did not appear to us that our greatest danger might still lie precisely in too long a continuation of the war, in the destruction of Europe's equilibrium, and in the sapping of the vital energies of the European peoples. It did not appear to us then that the greatest interest we had in the war was still that it should be brought to an end as soon as possible on a basis involving a minimum maladjustment and as much stability as possible for the future. Prior to our entry into the war, many people had thought that way. . . .

Considerations of the power balance argued against total victory. Perhaps it was for this very reason that people in this country rejected them so emphatically and sought more sweeping and grandiose objectives, for the accomplishment of which total victory could plausibly be represented as absolutely essential. In any case, a line of thought grew up, under Wilson's leadership, which provided both rationale and objective for our part in fighting the war to a bitter end. Germany was militaristic and antidemocratic. The Allies were fighting to make the world safe for democracy. Prussian militarism had to be destroyed to make way for the sort of peace we wanted. This peace would not be based on the old balance of power. Who, as Wilson said, could guarantee equilibrium under such a system? It would be based this time on a "community of power," on "an organized common peace," on a League of Nations which would mobilize the conscience and power of mankind against aggression. Autocratic government would be done away with. Peoples would themselves choose the sovereignty under which they wished to reside. Poland would achieve her independence, as would likewise the restless peoples of the Austro-Hungarian Empire. There would be open diplomacy this time; peoples, not governments, would run things. Armaments would be reduced by mutual agreement. The peace would be just and secure.

In the name of such principles you could fight a war to the end. A future so brilliant would surely wash away the follies and brutalities of the war, redress its injuries, heal the wounds it had left. . . . Under the protecting shadow of this theory the guns continued their terrible work for a final year and a half after our entry. Under the shadow of this theory Wilson went to Versailles unprepared to face the sordid but all-important details of the day of reckoning. Under this theory he suffered his tragic and historic failure. Under this theory things advanced with a deadly logic and precision to a peace which was indeed "forced upon the loser, a victor's terms imposed upon the vanquished, accepted in humiliation, under duress" —a peace that did indeed leave a sting, a resentment, a bitter memory, and upon which its own terms came later to rest "as upon quicksand."

And the tragedy of this outcome was not substantially mitigated by the fact that we were not signatories to the Treaty of Versailles and kept ourselves aloof from its punitive provisions. The damage had been done. The equilibrium of Europe had been shattered. Austria-Hungary was gone. There was nothing effective to take its place. Germany, smarting from the sting of defeat and plunged into profound social unrest by the breakup of her traditional institutions, was left nevertheless as the only great united state in Central Europe. Russia was no longer there, as a possible reliable ally, to help France contain German power. From the Russian plain there leered a single hostile eye, skeptical of Europe's values, rejoicing at all Europe's misfortunes, ready to collaborate solely for the final destruction of her spirit and her pride. Between Russia and Germany were only the pathetic new states of eastern and Central Europe, lacking in domestic stability and the traditions of statesmanship—their peoples bewildered, uncertain, vacillating between brashness and timidity in the exercise of the unaccustomed responsibilities of independence. And to the other side of Germany were France and England, reeling, themselves, from the vicissitudes of the war, wounded far more deeply than they themselves realized, the plume of their manhood gone, their world positions shaken. . . .

. . . The absence of a major war on the Continent during the century before 1914 had rested on a balance of power which presupposed the existence of France, Germany, Austria-Hungary, and Russia as dominant elements—and all of this flanked by an England instinctively conscious of her stake in the preservation of the balance among them and prepared to hover vigilantly about the fringes of the Continent, tending its equilibrium as one might tend a garden, yet always with due regard for the preservation of her own maritime supremacy and the protection of her overseas empire. In this complicated structure lay concealed not only the peace of Europe but also the security of the United States. Whatever affected it was bound to affect us. . . .

Now you could, it seems to me, have taken this view—so well substantiated by the subsequent course of events—as your point of departure, let us say, from 1913. You might then, departing from the recognition that serious troubles were brewing in Europe and that our interests were endangered, have seen to it that this country provided itself right then and there with something in the way of an armed establishment, so that our word would carry some weight and be listened to in the councils of the powers. When war broke out, you could have ignored the nonsensical timidities of technical neutrality and used our influence to achieve the earliest possible termination of a war that nobody could really win. . . . And if you finally had to intervene to save the British from final defeat (which I am quite prepared to accept as a valid ground for intervention), then you could have gone in frankly for the avowed purpose both of doing this and of ending the war as rapidly as possible; you could have refrained from moralistic slogans, refrained from picturing your effort as a crusade, kept open your lines of negotiation to the enemy, declined to break up his empires and overthrow his political system, avoided commitments to the extremist war aims of your allies, retained your freedom of action, exploited your bargaining power flexibly with a view to bringing its full weight to bear at the crucial moments in order to achieve the termination of hostilities with a minimum prejudice to the future stability of the Continent.

All these things, as I say, you might conceivably have done. If you ask me, "Can you guarantee that this would have produced a better outcome and a happier future?" my answer is, "Of course not." I can say only that I fail to see how it could have produced a much worse one. And I can say that it would have been a conceptual framework more closely related to the realities of the world we live in . . . .

But I think I hear one great, and even indignant, objection to what I have suggested; and I must speak to it before I close. People will say to me: You know that what you have suggested was totally impossible from the standpoint of public opinion; that people in general had no idea that our interests were affected by what was going on in Europe in 1913; that they would never have dreamed of spending real money for armaments in time of peace; that they would never have gone into a war deliberately, as a result of cold calculation about the balance of power elsewhere; that they would have made war only upon direct provocation; that they could never have been brought to forgive such provocation and to refrain from pressing such a war to its final conclusion. . . . You—these people will say to me—hold yourself out as a realist, and yet none of these things you are talking about were even ever within the realm of practical possibility from the standpoint of domestic realities in our own country.

I have no quarrel with this argument. I am even going to concede it. I do think that political leaders might have made greater efforts than they did, from time to time, to inform themselves and to tell people the true facts, and I think people might even have understood them and been grateful to them if they had. But let us let that go and say that basically the argument is sound. I still have one thing to say about it.

I am not talking here about the behavior of Woodrow Wilson or Colonel House or Robert Lansing. I am talking about the behavior of the United States of America. History does not forgive us our national mistakes because they are explicable in terms of our domestic politics. If you say that mistakes of the past were unavoidable because of our domestic predilections and habits of thought, you are saying that what stopped us from being more effective than we were was democracy, as practiced in this country. And, if that is true, let us recognize it and measure the full seriousness of it—and find something to do about it. A nation which excuses its own failures by the sacred untouchableness of its own habits can excuse itself into complete disaster. I said in the first of these lectures that the margin in which it is given to us to commit blunders has been drastically narrowed in the last fifty years. If it was the workings of our democracy that were inadequate in the past, let us say so. Whoever thinks the future is going to be easier than the past is certainly mad. And the system under which we are going to have to continue to conduct foreign policy, is, I hope and pray, the system of democracy.

PROBLEM 14

A War for Principles

Writers who stressed security and balance of power sharply criticized the idealists and Woodrow Wilson. However, in emphasizing the threat to American security, these writers may have tended to ignore or distort what was really in the minds of Wilson and the American people when the nation went to war in 1917.

George F. Kennan, who was involved in policy-making after World War II, tried to derive some practical lessons from the tragedies of World War I. Yet, it is important that the historian also try to understand the past as it *really* was. In the case of the World War I era, he must judge Wilson's policies in terms of the problems facing the President then, as well as the relevance of those policies to the present, and he must try to discern how the American people felt in 1917.

Public opinion seemed solidly behind the President in his decision to go to war. If most Americans were not gripped by fear of the German threat to their security, as some of the realist writers claim, they must have been guided by other motives. For a number of reasons Americans had come to believe that the Allied cause was just and the German cause was evil. Disillusionment after the war blinded Americans to the fact that, *at the time,* they responded in a simple, moralistic way. They had been aroused to a strong and deep hostility toward the Germans. The stories of German atrocities in Belgium, although greatly exaggerated by the British, were widely believed at the time. Furthermore, the sinking of the *Lusitania* made a profound impression on the American mind and was almost universally regarded as a barbaric act.

Although they feared and dreaded war, Americans were willing to take a stand against the German military machine. By April 1917 they had come to believe that fundamental American values, which they knew to be right, were being challenged by a savage aggressor. A mad dog was loose and must be restrained. As President Wilson put it, "The world must be made safe for democracy."

In the reading for Problem 14, Robert H. Ferrell, a diplomatic historian, re-examines the question of motivation concerning the entry of the United States into World War I. His explanation of why the American people reacted to submarine warfare as they did opens another line of analysis.

As you read the excerpt from Ferrell's book, keep the following questions in mind:

1 Some writers have argued that military preparedness, including the possession of large standing armies, has been responsible to some extent for countries becoming involved in a war. In the United States, Ferrell says, military weakness contributed to its entry into World War I. Is there a contradiction here?

2 Ferrell says there is no proof that Wilson acted contrary to the wishes of the American people. By this token, does it prove that Wilson acted in accordance with their wishes?

3 Did the domestic situation in Germany justify using immoral means in warfare? Are standards of morality in international affairs less demanding than those which apply to domestic affairs?

4 Would the United States have stayed out of World War I if the *Lusitania* incident, which Ferrell describes as accidental, had not occurred? Do you think that the German submarine attacks would have aroused American moral outrage if there had been no United States citizens among the victims?

5 Ferrell equates the overwhelming vote of Congress in favor of entering World War I with the voice of the American people. Is it necessarily true that the wishes of the American people were reflected by the action of Congress?

6 How does the Ferrell reading differ in approach from that of George F. Kennan in Problem 13?

EMOTION, MORALITY, AND WORLD WAR I

The book from which the following reading is taken is a survey of American foreign policy from the American Revolution to 1959. In the excerpt printed here, Robert H. Ferrell discusses President Wilson's foreign policy and public opinion in America. ☐ Reprinted from *American Diplomacy, A History* by Robert H. Ferrell. By permission of W. W. Norton & Company, Inc. Copyright © 1959 by W. W. Norton & Company, Inc.

In retrospect there is no doubt that Germany's submarine measures, above anything else, brought the United States into the first World War in 1917. If the German government had used some other means of warfare against the Allies it seems certain that the United States would not have entered the war. This is not to say that the submarine issue alone antagonized the Americans, that there were no other issues on which the American people took issue with the Germans, but that the submarine issue was crucial in the American decision for war.

At the beginning of the war in 1914 the German government had blundered badly, so far as American opinion was concerned, by invading Belgium contrary to a solemn treaty of guarantee which Germany had signed. Americans were incensed by this act. Emotional and moralistic, they saw this attack by Germany on a weak neighbor, contrary to treaty, as a moral atrocity. The treaty of guarantee was admittedly old, almost a dead letter, negotiated in 1839, but it was a treaty and not a "scrap of paper" as the German chancellor, Theobald von Bethmann-Hollweg, described it to the British ambassador when the latter asked for his passports. Germany violated the treaty over the protests of the Belgians, whose King Albert is credited with an epigram when asked if the German troops could march through his country: "Belgium is a nation, not a thoroughfare." The Germans had marched, Belgium had futilely declared war, and the Belgian army after a stout defense had fallen back into northern France.

A German occupation followed in Belgium, and during its four years the Germans used the harshest measures to keep the restive Belgian population in order. . . . They executed some 5,000 Belgian civilians, some in large groups, chosen indiscriminately as hostages for Belgian good behavior. Whenever some German soldier was shot down by Belgian patriots the Germans retaliated by shooting hostages. If the more lurid atrocity stories . . . contained little truth, there remained this execution of hostages which, although perhaps militarily justifiable, was humanely outrageous. To the sensitive public opinion in America, an opinion highly idealistic, German occupation policy in Belgium was unspeakably reprehensible.

. . . May 7, 1915, was the date of the most shocking episode of the entire period 1914–1917, the sinking by a German submarine of the *Lusitania,* pride of the British merchant marine, largest and swiftest vessel on the transatlantic run. The Germans early in 1915 had announced their war zone around the British Isles, and this entailed sinking not merely warships and cargo ships but also liners. The Allies refused to believe that German submarines would attack the largest liners. There was a technical basis for such reasoning: until the *Lusitania* went down, the Germans had not been able to sink any vessel traveling faster than fourteen knots; because the liners were swift vessels it was deemed improbable that they could be attacked. And they possessed watertight bulkheads which presumably would minimize loss of life if they were attacked. Unfortunately, and contrary to such reasoning, Captain Turner of the *Lusitania* disobeyed his instructions as his ship came within sight of the Irish coast (he slowed down his vessel and refrained from zigzagging). Thus Commander Schwieger of the *U–20* managed (the following is from his ship's log) to get a sight on "four funnels and two masts of a steamer . . . Ship is made out to be large passenger steamer. . . . Clean bow shot at a distance of 700 meters . . . Torpedo hits starboard side right behind the bridge. An unusually heavy explosion takes place with a very strong explosion cloud (cloud reaches far beyond front funnel). The explosion of the torpedo must have been followed by a second one (boiler or coal or powder?). . . . The ship stops immediately and heels over to starboard very quickly, immersing simultaneously at the bow . . . the name *Lusitania* becomes visible in golden letters." With this act of inhumanity—1,198 people drowned, including 128 Americans—Germany committed one of the cardinal errors of the war.

No one remembered that the German authorities, in newspaper advertisements, had warned prospective passengers that the *Lusitania* was deemed subject to attack. No matter that the German emperor on June 6, after the *Lusitania* sinking, issued secret orders to his submarine commanders not to attack liners without warning, and that after an accidental attack on the British liner *Arabic* the German ambassador in the United States, although without authorization, made the imperial orders public. The American people were horrified at the sinking of the largest Atlantic liner. "Damnable! Damnable! Absolutely hellish!" cried the evangelist Billy Sunday.

More than any other single factor, Commander Schwieger's chance torpedo shot (he had, incidentally, almost finished his cruise; it was his last torpedo) hurt the German cause in America. The American people were incensed at Germany and with almost one voice supported the Wilson administration's diplomatic protests. . . . There was never, to be sure, any serious possibility of America going to war over the *Lusitania* outrage. The country was unready for such action, but it was ready for the strongest diplomatic protests.

The German case thus suffered in the United States because of the Belgian invasion and occupation and the sinking of the *Lusitania*. These acts were monumental instances of the German policy of *Schrecklichkeit* (frightfulness). There were other irritations, such as the crude attempts to sabotage American war industry which in December 1915 resulted in expulsion from the country of the German military and naval attaches, Captains Franz von Papen and Karl Boy-Ed. The Austrian ambassador in the United States, who bore the unfortunate name of Dumba, was also expelled after the British secret service intercepted and published some compromising correspondence, showing that he had been privy to schemes for fomenting strikes in munitions factories. Then there were the continuing incidents over German submarine warfare. After sinking of the *Lusitania* there was a lull as the Germans abandoned for the moment their unrestricted submarine tactics, but early in 1916 they again undertook all-out submarine warfare and a new crisis arose when a submarine sank the *Sussex* on March 24, 1916. President Wilson gave the German government a virtual ultimatum in the matter of unrestricted submarine warfare—that if the Germans used it again, a third time, the United States would break diplomatic relations. The German government for the moment backed down, and relations between Washington and Berlin became relatively placid for the rest of the year 1916, until the crisis of January 1917. . . .

. . . [During this time] President Wilson undertook a mediation of the war, an effort to bring to an end in Europe what had become a terrible slaughter, and to end it with, as Wilson described his purposes, a peace without victory. . . .

Nothing resulted from this pacific effort. . . .

After the presidential elections in the United States, Wilson made a final mediation effort. . . . The Allies obliged by asking for a settlement that the German government would not accept . . . . After much prodding the Germans confidentially communicated terms to Wilson, but these were as impossible as those of the Allies . . . . At the same time they revealed their peace terms, the German government on January 31, 1917, sent word through Ambassador Johann von Bernstorff of a new unrestricted submarine campaign.

The German admiralty had concluded that there was an excellent chance of knocking Britain out of the war by a blockade of the British Isles, the blockade including not merely munitions but everything, particularly food coming to Britain from the United States, India, and Argentina (especially the latter two countries, for harvests in the United States had been poor in 1916). The admiralty and the leaders of the German general staff knew that unrestricted submarine warfare would bring the United States into the conflict on the side of the Allies, but they were prepared to take this chance. They knew that American armaments were almost entirely naval. Great Britain controlled the seas anyway, and if the American fleet were added to the British it would make little difference in the outcome of the war. The American peacetime army was of no military importance, and they calculated that before the United States could raise, equip, and train a great army, let alone transport it across the Atlantic, the war would be over. If the United States in 1917 had possessed a dozen ready army divisions the German government might well have hesitated. The United States did not have the ready army divisions, and [German] Admiral Eduard von Capelle, [Admiral Alfred von] Tirpitz's successor as minister of marine, declared in the Reichstag that the military significance of American intervention would be "zero, zero, zero!" The unrestricted submarine campaign began on February 1, and on February 3 Wilson severed diplomatic relations.

Between the breaking of relations and the declaration of war there was a lapse of two months during which Wilson and the country determined on a course of action. War was not inevitable even after Bernstorff received his passport, for the nation could have followed a course of armed neutrality. Wilson seems to have wavered during this crucial period, waiting until Germany had given unmistakable indication of how seriously she would take the protests of the United States over her violations of neutral rights and, generally, her conduct of the war.

Wilson conceivably had armed neutrality in view when during February he asked Congress for authority to arm American merchant ships. He was not given it; in the Senate a "little group of willful men" by filibuster kept the bill from coming to a vote before the Sixty-fourth Congress ended on March 4 under the then law.

Meantime, the course for the American government became clear. A German submarine on February 25 sank the Cunard liner *Laconia;* it was the *Lusitania* all over again. This news came to the White House almost simultaneously with intelligence of the Zimmermann Note, in which the German foreign secretary, Alfred Zimmermann, sought to entice the Mexican government into war, not yet declared, with the United States, promising that Mexico might "reconquer the lost territory in New Mexico, Texas, and Arizona." This incredible missive incensed President Wilson because it had been transmitted to Mexico from Berlin via the American embassy in

Berlin and the State Department in Washington. Because of British control of the cables Wilson had allowed the Germans to use American channels; the Germans had used them to transmit a hostile message. American newspapers published the Zimmermann Note on March 1.

Wilson called Congress into special session. The Senate arranged to limit debate, but now it was asked to declare war rather than mere armed neutrality. President Wilson delivered his war message to Congress in person on April 2; the joint resolution declaring war was passed on April 6, with overwhelming majorities.

To report these events does not altogether explain the official and popular decision for war. The reasons which took the United States to war in 1917 have been and will continue to be examined, questioned, and debated.

There had been the major issue of neutral rights between the United States and Germany, and this had brought the break in relations in February 1917. The issue had been presented to Americans in a startlingly graphic and poignant manner in the *Lusitania* disaster, and it is safe to say that nearly two years later, in early 1917, the sinking of the great liner was still in most American minds a large mark against the German cause. The Germans had refused to state publicly their war aims, and had followed their refusal by a third declaration of unrestricted submarine warfare.

There was the German invasion of Belgium and the severe and oppressive occupation policy of the Germans in that country.

There was the Zimmermann Note.

Also, while the decision was making, the issue of good versus bad was somewhat clarified by the first Russian revolution of March 12, 1917. The tsarist power was overthrown and a republic set up (this lasted until November 1917, when the Bolsheviks overthrew it). The Russian republic of March was substituted in the Allied coalition for an embarrassingly autocratic member and the change strengthened the feeling of Americans that the Allies were fighting the despotisms of Central Europe.

There were historical traditions and attitudes. It was easy for the people of the United States to recognize at this crucial time the tie of common language and kinship between America and Great Britain, to remember the somewhat neglected revolutionary bond between the United States and France.

There was also the trade in munitions and foodstuffs, the economic ties between the United States and the Allies. Despite the increased stringency of Allied measures and German countermeasures in 1914–1917, American foreign trade had by no means been eliminated. Trade with the Allies increased dramatically and took on the characteristics of a boom. Prosperity

singleness of purpose at April 6, 1917 (the Congress vote in favor of war was overwhelming, 82–6 in the Senate, 373–50 in the House) was a view of balance of power, but not the traditional view. The decision in 1917 was emotional, grounded in the belief, indeed conviction, that right, in the person of the Allies, was battling wrong, personified by the Central Powers. There was abroad, so Wilson and his fellow Americans believed, a concerted, highly organized, brutal, savage campaign against decency and morality, and in the early spring of 1917 evil was weighing heavily in the balance against good. The American people, having enjoyed throughout their history an abundant life in a material sense, having from their own successes come to believe that their principles were correct principles, lacking bitterness and cynicism about the motives and behavior of foreign peoples, were willing to take a stand against what most students even today would grant was a ruthless German military ambition. The American people, to the entire disbelief of contemporary foreign observers and to the disbelief of their own children of the next generation, were willing to take a stand in the world for principle. Americans in the long months of neutrality, from 1914 to 1917, had come to feel that their principles were being challenged. "The world," Wilson said in his war message, "must be made safe for democracy."

PROBLEM 15

World War I: A Survey

Thus far Unit Three has presented views of the revisionists, the idealists, the realists, and the moralists. Among other theories dealing with causes of World War I is that of Arthur S. Link, editor of "The Papers of Woodrow Wilson" and biographer of the President. Link expressed the belief that Mr. Wilson was faced with such complex domestic and foreign pressures that his problems were virtually insolvable. His view might be called the "tragic dilemma" concept because it suggests that President Wilson had no alternative but to involve the United States in World War I.

Ernest R. May, a specialist in twentieth-century American diplomatic history, discusses the tragic-dilemma view in the reading for Problem 15 while offering a survey of major interpretations. Presented with premises that the war was either a great crusade or a horrible mistake, the student is challenged to examine American entry into the war objectively and realistically and to arrive at his own conclusions. By so doing he will be utilizing skills most necessary for the historian.

In reading the selection by May, keep the following questions in mind:

1 What do the revisionists and the realists have in common in their interpretations? What do they have in common as historians?

2 Is the tragic-dilemma theory similar to the concept that the Civil War was the product of a "blundering generation"?

3 From this reading, what support could you give to the argument that the United States might just as logically have declared war against the British?

4 Ernest R. May states that political scientists have approached the question of World War I causation differently from the historians. If this conclusion is correct, why should it be so?

5 Which interpretation or combination of interpretations is the most convincing to you?

AMERICAN INTERVENTION IN 1917

Ernest R. May analyzes various interpretations of American involvement in World War I and presents his own. □ Ernest R. May, *American Intervention: 1917 and 1941*, pp. 1–11. Washington, D.C.: Service Center for Teachers of History. Copyright © 1960 by The American Historical Association.

In the Soviet Union, "peace-loving" is an epithet [used] exclusively for socialist nations. "Aggressive capitalist-imperialist" countries are supposed not to deserve it. On the historical record, however, it probably fits the American people more than almost any other, for the United States has been the home of most modern peace movements, including those for international arbitration and universal disarmament. Until very recently, the nation characteristically followed aggressively isolationist foreign policies and stood ostentatiously unprepared for war. Americans seemed not only to love peace but to be infatuated with it. And not least among evidences of this romantic spirit was the guilt feeling that seemed to sweep the land after each of its wars. Bitter self-recrimination followed the Mexican War, the Civil War, the Spanish-American War, and especially the two World Wars.

In historical writing, it is true, the reaction has usually been slow. After World War I, according to most observers, disillusionment quickly settled over the public. Through most of the 1920's, nevertheless, hard cover books dealing with the war continued to express pride and satisfaction in American intervention. The most widely read histories of it were two semi-autobiographies: *The Life and Letters of Walter H. Page* (3 volumes; Garden City, 1922–26), edited by Burton J. Hendrick, and *The Intimate Papers of Colonel House* (4 volumes; Boston, 1926–28), edited by Charles Seymour. Page had been American ambassador in London, and House, who was still alive [when his papers were published], had been President Wilson's confidant and unofficial ambassador-at-large. According to the extracts from their diaries and letters published in these volumes, both had advocated intervention and rejoiced that it had taken place. Though both works consisted mainly of raw materials for history rather than history itself, they did lay down guidelines for one interpretation of Wilson's diplomacy.

They both divided the 1914–17 years, roughly speaking, into two periods, broken by the "Lusitania" crisis of May-June, 1915. In the first period, according to both Page-Hendrick and House-Seymour, the moral imperative to intervene was not yet obvious. The issue at that time was simply whether or not the United States would obstruct the Allies. Wilson and his official aides, Secretary of State William Jennings Bryan and State Department Counselor Robert Lansing, inclined to be overly legalistic. In particular, they pressed for acceptance by the belligerents of the unratified Declaration of London of 1909, a code of rules for naval warfare which, by protecting American trade with continental Europe, would have seriously limited the Allies' ability to cut off food and supplies for Germany. Page fought this policy of his government with all his resources. On one occasion he visited the foreign secretary, Sir Edward Grey, read him a formal note from the State Department, and then said, "I have now read the despatch, but I do not agree with it; let us consider how it should be answered!" House meanwhile carried on the same battle in Washington, quietly advising Wilson and going behind the back of the State Department to work out a compromise with the British ambassador. The United States eventually gave up the Declaration of London. Both Page-Hendrick and House-Seymour celebrate this victory as the first among many that kept the United States from getting in the way of the Allies.

In the second phase, after the "Lusitania" sinking, according to both works, benevolent neutrality ceased to be enough. Page had actually become convinced earlier that German militarism represented a threat to American democracy; House had had twinges of the same conviction. After the spring of 1915, Page rarely doubted that it was his country's duty to get into the war as soon as possible. House urged breaking relations with Germany. When Wilson allowed the "Lusitania" issue to cool, House advised that the next submarine incident, the sinking of the "Arabic" in August, 1915, be made occasion for the break. He made the same plea after an attack on the Channel steamer, "Sussex," in the spring of 1916. At moments of crisis, House and Page were together in urging that opportunity be seized for a rupture in relations or a declaration of war.

House meanwhile was recommending that Wilson plan for possible intervention. In the winter of 1915/16 he induced the President to send him to Europe on an extraordinary mission. With Wilson's approval, he was to seek an agreement with the Allies under which Wilson would make a public appeal for peace negotiations. If the Germans either refused or, accepting, declined to meet conditions satisfactory to the Allies, the United States would then intervene. This agreement was actually initialled by House and Grey in February, 1916, and endorsed conditionally by Wilson. Owing to circumstance, it was never put into effect. Wilson made a public appeal in December, 1916, but only after telling House that the agreement with Britain was out of date. House regarded the President's peace move as a mistake which happily came to nought. And in 1917 the President finally yielded, broke relations, and asked Congress to declare war on Germany.

Underlying both the Page and House accounts was the contention that American intervention was desirable and prudent, at least after the "Lusitania" sinking, if not before. Their reasoning was partly moralistic. Germany was taken to represent absolutism and aggressive militarism, a nation whose principles were antithetic [directly opposed] to those of the United States and the western Allies. From this premise, the war seemed a test of which code, which set of political abstractions, would prevail. The United States had to join in preventing a German victory in order to defend representative government, individual freedom, and the bourgeois virtues. Imperial Germany was a malignant survival of feudalism, and it needed to be destroyed if the world were to be made safe for democracy.

But the Page-Hendrick and House-Seymour view drew on another line of reasoning, one occasionally articulated at the time and put forward later by Walter Lippmann in *U.S. Foreign Policy: Shield of the Republic* (Boston: Little, Brown, 1943). The argument in this case was that the security of the United States depended on there being no dominant power in Europe. Wilhelminian Germany, like Napoleonic France, threatened to master all the continent's immense war potential. Britain would be unable to stand against such a menace, and the United States would confront an enemy stronger than itself, not only capable of challenging its hemispheric supremacy but of jeopardizing its very existence. As Page and House hinted and Lippmann, among others, later said explicitly, the United States had a vital security interest in helping the Allies to prevent German triumph.

It was only toward the end of the 1920's that numerous publicists and scholars began to chip at the justificatory reasoning of the Page and House accounts. Part of the attack was indirect. Americans joined Englishmen and Germans in re-examining the wartime assumption that Germany had been responsible for starting the war. A revised image of imperial Germany emerged from the forty volumes of [*Die*] *Diplomatischen Akten des Aus-*

wärtigen Amtes, 1871–1914 ["The Diplomatic Acts of the Foreign Office, 1871–1914"], better known as *Die Grosse Politik,* and this new image was not altogether consistent with the moral premise of American intervention. Bickerings among erstwhile allies, coupled with the consolidation of Soviet power and the rise of Fascism in Italy, made it seem doubtful if the war had in fact made democracy any safer. The color of disillusionment began to seep into publishers' lists and the pages of learned journals.

In 1929 C. Hartley Grattan, an Australian-born journalist, published in New York a detailed indictment of Wilson's diplomacy entitled *Why We Fought.* Contending that neither the United States nor the world had gained anything from the war, he asked how and why America had abandoned neutrality. He condemned Wilson for giving up the Declaration of London and receding from his initial stand against private loans to belligerent governments. He blamed both decisions first on the sentimental Anglophilism of Page, House, and Wilson as well, and second on the influence of capitalists, financiers, and munitions makers who profited from supplying the Allies. He argued that Wilson had taken a stand against German submarine warfare more because it menaced trade than because it threatened neutral rights, and that he had pressed his case to the point of rupture and finally war in order to protect America's investment in the Allied cause. Grattan charged the President with practically plotting to bring on intervention, citing tendentious testimony from a senile congressman that Wilson had called a "sunrise conference" early in 1916 to tell Congressional leaders that he wanted war. In explaining Wilson's eventual request for a declaration of war, Grattan laid great stress on a telegram from Page in which the Ambassador warned that Britain faced economic collapse if America did not enter the war. And the public followed the President, Grattan contended, because it had been barraged with English propaganda and frightened by administration-contrived tales of German espionage and sabotage. This crude summary does not do justice to Grattan's skillfully argued indictment, any more than the preceding summary did justice to the Page-Hendrick and House-Seymour volumes, but Grattan did put forward all the themes that were to course through later disillusionist writing. He charged the administration with having worked in the interest of munition makers and bankers, and he contended that the people had been tricked into an irrational and almost hysterical frame of mind.

These views won wide belief during the Great Depression. In 1936 and 1937, Ray Stannard Baker, who had worked with Wilson at Versailles and later, reached the neutrality years in volumes V and VI of his eight-volume authorized biography. Despite his continuing reverence for Wilson,

Baker assailed the follies of Page and House, deplored the dropping of the Declaration of London, ridiculed the House-Grey understanding, and lamented the final decision to intervene. Walter Millis of the *New York Herald Tribune* meanwhile devoted his lively pen and studious mind to a one volume account of the background of intervention, *Road to War, 1914-1917* (Boston: Houghton Mifflin, 1935). A popular best-seller, Millis's book also poked sardonic fun at the illusions of the interventionists and suggested that the event itself had been due to a combination of folly, sentimentalism, and greed. In 1936 the United States Senate set up a special committee under the chairmanship of Senator Gerald P. Nye of North Dakota to investigate the influence of munitions makers on foreign policy. The committee interrogated representatives of such firms as J. P. Morgan and Company and the National City Bank of New York and ransacked the files of the State and Treasury Departments. Various international lawyers, notably Edwin M. Borchard of Yale and the elderly John Bassett Moore, had meanwhile opened crusades against the legal theories upon which Wilson had acted. Borchard and William P. Lage published *Neutrality for the United States* (New Haven: Yale U. Press, 1937). And the results of this work, other lawyers' essays, Baker's biography, Millis's book, the Nye committee hearings, and the climate of the times were the successive neutrality acts . . . .

. . . Charles Callan Tansill's *America Goes to War* (Boston: Little, Brown, 1938), gave the disillusionist view of intervention its ultimate scholarly distillation. Eventually a professor at Fordham University and then at Georgetown University, Tansill had previously published monographs on American relations with Santo Domingo and on the acquisition of the Virgin Islands. Though not allowed to use the Wilson manuscripts, which Baker still hoarded, he had seen parts of the unpublished House diaries, and he had been given free rein among the gatherings of the Nye Committee. He had correspondence from an obliging officer in the Berlin Marine-Archiv which enabled him to sketch the German side. His bibliography, though including some items not actually used, was full and impressive.

Tansill's volume stressed the enormous growth of American trade in munitions and other war supplies and the extent of American private loans to the Allies. Portraying House, Page, and even Lansing as influenced by these interests and moved by blind hatred for Germany, he showed how they frustrated true neutrality, as he conceived it, persuading the President to abandon the Declaration of London, give up his early opposition to loans, resist pressure for an arms embargo, and take an unjustifiable stand against German submarine warfare. Some of the chapter titles indicate the thread of argument: "III. War Profits Beckon to 'Big Business'," "VI. England

Looks Upon the Declaration of London As a 'Mere Scrap of Paper'," "XI. Mr. Lansing Leads the President Along the Road to War," "XV. Colonel House Blocks a Path to Peace," "XVIII. The Kaiser Chooses Peace with America Rather Than Victory at Verdun." Though reviewers in scholarly journals did not call his book dispassionate, most found it . . . convincing.

The interpretation popularized by Grattan and Millis and footnoted by Tansill had, of course, its own foundation in faith. It rested on the premise that the United States had had no reason, moral or material, for opposing Germany or helping the Allies. Some members of this school assumed that if the United States had remained neutral a negotiated peace would have resulted, with happier results than those of the Versailles *Diktat*. Even if Germany had been absolutist, militaristic, and imperialistic, which these writers doubted, and even if it had been on the edge of triumph, still they felt that the outcome of the war should have remained a matter of indifference to Americans. As many writers asserted, among them Charles A. Beard in his eloquent *Open Door at Home* (New York: Macmillan, 1934), the United States was strong precisely because it did not involve itself in European power politics and waste itself in diplomatic chicanery and preparations for war. From this premise it followed as night the day that the intervention of 1917 had been at least a blunder and probably a crime.

Though most writing on the 1914–17 years had fallen into this category or the other, represented by Page's *Letters* and the House *Papers,* another approach had also been evident all along. In 1923 Malbone W. Graham published a University of Texas Ph.D. thesis entitled *The Controversy Between the United States and Allied Governments Respecting Neutral Rights and Commerce During the Period of American Neutrality, 1914–1917* (Austin: U. of Texas, 1923). In it there was neither glorification of American policy nor recrimination against its architects. Graham found that with slight departures in one direction or another the United States had tried to follow the applicable rules of international law. Another young scholar, Richard Van Alstyne, writing in the *Journal of Modern History* for 1935 reached much the same conclusion about the abandonment of the Declaration of London. But, curiously enough, it was Charles Seymour, the editor of the House *Papers,* who published the first book-length study dealing with intervention as a historical episode rather than a question of moral doctrine.

In *American Diplomacy during the World War* (Baltimore: Johns Hopkins U. Press, 1934), the Albert Shaw lectures for 1933, and in supplementary essays published as *American Neutrality, 1914–1917* (New Haven: Yale U. Press, 1935), Seymour analyzed the principal lines of Wilson's diplomacy: his policies toward the Allies, his efforts to mediate, and his opposition to the submarine. In the first case, he found that while the President and his advisers were influenced by belief in the moral superiority of the English and French, they also adhered to international law as they understood it and, indeed, risked serious friction with the Allies in order to prevent inroads upon it. Seymour pointed out that in the interval between the "Sussex" pledge [in which Germany replied on May 4, 1916 to Wilson's ultimatum of April 18] and the coming of war, when German submarines were under control, American relations with Britain were more troubled than those with Germany. Wilson even talked vexedly of employing economic sanctions against the Allies.

The submarine issue alone, Seymour contended, brought intervention. Wilson saw with increasing clarity that German undersea warfare represented a moral challenge. If a belligerent could extend its operations anywhere, interfere with the trade of neutral states, and imperil the lives of neutral citizens, then neither neutrality nor international law possessed meaning. In conscience, the President felt compelled to oppose the Germans on this issue and, paradoxically, to risk neutrality for the sake of neutrality. He was not entirely altruistic, for American lives and property were those mainly at stake. Though the German government respected Wilson's wishes for a time, it eventually ceased to do so. At Spa on January 7, 1917, the Kaiser and his advisers decided to launch an unrestricted submarine campaign in defiance of the United States and in conscious certainty that war would result. Wilson saw the challenge as one he could not evade. . . .

After World War II a generation with different attitudes and preoccupations began to restudy problems of World War I. Lippmann had already provided them with one new point of departure by suggesting that intervention had been necessary for the rescue of the balance of power and the protection of American security. In various popular and scholarly periodicals and in a book, *In Defense of the National Interest* (New York: Knopf, 1951), a University of Chicago political scientist, Hans J. Morgenthau, attacked the Wilson administration for having failed to concentrate on realistic goals. In 1950, in lectures printed as *American Diplomacy, 1900–1950* (Chicago: U. of Chicago Press, 1950), the erudite and sophisticated career diplomat, George Frost Kennan, put the same charge into captivating phrases. He accused Wilson and other American leaders of excessive moralism and legalism. Taking a position halfway between the major prewar schools, he argued that while intervention might have been justified by the national interest, the overlay of other excuses had ruined its purpose. . . .

The questions posed by this analysis of American policy intrigued a number of young scholars. Robert E. Osgood, a political scientist in Morgenthau's Chicago Center for the Study of American Foreign Policy, investigated them in *Ideals and Self-Interest in America's Foreign Relations* (Chicago: U. of Chicago Press, 1953). In several chapters devoted to World War I, he amplified the theses that Morgenthau and Kennan had sketched. Another political scientist, Edward H. Buehrig of the University of Indiana, in *Woodrow Wilson and the Balance of Power* (Bloomington: Indiana U. Press, 1955), suggested that these criticisms were not altogether fair. The submarine issue symbolized a clash of national interests, he said, and while American leaders did concern themselves with legal and moral issues, Wilson, House, and especially Lansing showed acute awareness of the balance of power. While the two prewar schools had argued over whether the intervention was right or wrong, this postwar group asked if it might not have been right for the wrong reasons.

Meanwhile, like the tortoise competing with the hare, the separate line of scholarship started by Graham, Van Alstyne, and Seymour had kept up its plodding pace. Arthur S. Link, Professor of History at Princeton, Northwestern, and then Princeton again, launched a magisterial [or authoritative] biography of Wilson, of which the three stout volumes already published [Princeton, 1947, 1956, 1960] carry the President only to the "Arabic" crisis of 1915. [A fourth volume was published in 1964.] In a shorter work, *Woodrow Wilson and the Progressive Era* (New York: Harper, 1954), and in *Wilson the Diplomatist* (Baltimore: Johns Hopkins U. Press, 1957), the Albert Shaw lectures for 1956, Link sketched his tentative findings, pointing out the domestic problems that Wilson faced, the power of the near-pacifist group within his own party and the significance of the Progressive and pro-preparedness blocs which he had either to conquer or capture. Link portrayed Wilson as a man of many-sided thought, at once a realist and a moralist, wrestling with extremely complex issues. Like Seymour, Link suggested that the range of alternatives actually open to Wilson was much narrower than either the Page-House, the isolationist, or the Morgenthau-Kennan schools had acknowledged.

This same thesis characterized my own *The World War and American Isolation* (Cambridge: Harvard U. Press, 1959). In that book, I argued that in nearly every case requiring a decision by the President, there were present considerations of law, morality, power, national prestige, and domestic politics, all of which had to be taken into account. Neither Wilson nor his advisers could ever see very clearly the probable results of their decisions. In each instance, the weight of argument seemed to commend the course finally adopted. Each time, however, the decision tended to close out one or more alternatives until in 1917 there seemed no real option except war. The Germans, whom I tried to study in some detail, found themselves similarly driven into a corner from which they could see no exit save war. Link and I and a few others, notably William L. Langer in two essays in *Woodrow Wilson and the World Today* (Philadelphia: U. of Pa. Press, 1957), have tended to put aside the probably insoluble question of whether intervention was good or bad and simply to set forth the tragic dilemmas in which the men of 1917 found themselves. It is perhaps significant that most of those who continue the moral debate on World War I are men who call themselves political scientists. Historians have come by and large to deal with World War I much as with the Punic or Napoleonic wars.

Biographies

Following are brief biographical sketches of historians, educators, statesmen, and writers whose works are discussed in *The Causes of War*. Excerpts from the writings or reports of eighteen of these men comprise the readings in this volume.

ANDREWS, CHARLES McLEAN (1863–1943), historian. Andrews' interest in American colonialism developed when he was a student of Herbert B. Adams at Johns Hopkins University. It was stimulated further by his teaching experience at Bryn Mawr College, Johns Hopkins, and Yale. He was an historian of the British Empire, and although he was critical of the Bancroft patriotic historians, he did see weaknesses in the British imperial policy. His works include *The Old English Manor* (1892); *The Colonial Background of the American Revolution* (1924); and *The Colonial Period of American History* (1934–1938), the first volume of which won him the 1935 Pulitzer Prize for history. (Problems 2, 3, 5)

BANCROFT, GEORGE (1800–1891), historian and diplomat, mastered four languages while studying in Europe in order to read historical manuscripts in the original language. President Polk appointed him Secretary of the Navy in 1845, and while at that post Bancroft established the Naval Academy at Annapolis. Bancroft's chronicles are colorful, and his works include *A History of the United States of America, from the Discovery of the Continent* (1834–1874) and *The History of the Formation of the Constitution of the United States* (1882). (Problems 1, 5)

BEARD, CHARLES AUSTIN (1874–1948), historian, was at one time considered a radical, chiefly as a result of his book *An Economic Interpretation of the Constitution* (1913). The adverse comments it brought influenced him to enter public administration in 1917, and in this field he won recognition for his work in Tokyo. Beard served on the faculty at Columbia University and at Johns Hopkins. With his wife, Mary Ritter Beard, he wrote *The Rise of American Civilization* (1927), and during the administration of President Franklin D. Roosevelt, he was a severe critic of the New Deal. His books include *Basic History of the United States* (1944); *American Foreign Policy in the Making, 1932–1940* (1946); and *President Roosevelt and the Coming of the War, 1941* (1948). (Problems 2, 5, 6, 10, 15)

BECKER, CARL LOTUS (1873–1945), historian. An association with Frederick Jackson Turner, a history professor at the University of Wisconsin, prompted Becker to re-evaluate his views on historical research. He became fascinated with the power of the "perceiving mind of the historian" and won a reputation in both European and American history. Among his works are *The Heavenly City of the Eighteenth-Century Philosophers* (1932), a short study of French pre-revolution intellectuals, and *Political Parties in the Province of New York from 1760–1775* (1908), a discussion of the background of the American Revolution. (Problems 2, 5)

BEER, GEORGE LOUIS (1872–1920), historian and publicist. Beer's association with Herbert Levi Osgood at Columbia University stimulated his interest in colonial history, particularly that of the British Empire. He treated English colonialism sympathetically, arguing that it benefited both the mother country and the colonies. While working as a correspondent during World War I, Beer promoted favorable Anglo-American relations and later was appointed by Woodrow Wilson to "The Inquiry" committee, which studied the problems of composing a peace treaty. His writings include *Cromwell's Policy in Its Economic Aspects* (1902); *British Colonial Policy, 1754–1765* (1907); and *Origins of the British Colonial System, 1578–1660* (1908). (Problem 5)

CRAVEN, AVERY ODELLE (1886–), historian. Craven's Quaker ancestors migrated to the Middle West from the South because of their opposition to slavery. Craven grew up and spent all his school years through college in Iowa, later receiving degrees from Harvard, the University of Chicago, and Cambridge. He taught at the University of Chicago from 1928 to 1954, and later at various universities both in the United States and abroad. He joined the faculty of the University of Wisconsin in 1964. His writings include *The Repressible Conflict* (1939); *The Coming of the Civil War* (1942); and *The United States, Experiment in Democracy* (1947). (Problems 8, 9, 10)

DAVIDSON, PHILIP GRANT (1902–), historian and educator. The sense of accomplishment derived from tutoring while in high school and college convinced Davidson that he wanted to become a teacher, and the books on history in his father's library were an influence in his choice of a teaching field. While an instructor at Agnes Scott College, he helped coordinate the activities of four colleges and universities located around Atlanta, Georgia. Later, he became President of the University of Louisville. Davidson has written *Propaganda and the American Revolution, 1763–1783* (1941). (Problem 4)

DICKERSON, OLIVER MORTON (1875–), historian. In 1937, while examining British records on the Navigation Acts and on taxation, Dickerson discovered documents, now more than two hundred years old, which were thought to have been lost. As a result, authentic files and records of custom houses in American and English ports were made available to scholars. They also furnished material for Dickerson's book *The Navigation Acts and the American Revolution* (1951). *American Colonial Government, 1696–1765* (1962) was written after Dickerson had explored extensive records in the United States and in England. (Problem 5)

FERRELL, ROBERT HUGH (1921–), historian and educator. The pyramids which Ferrell saw while he was stationed in Egypt during World War II intrigued him so much that he changed his education major from music to history when he returned to Bowling Green State University in 1945. In 1962 he was appointed director of the Lilly Endowment in American history, a research program for teachers, at Indiana University. His books include *Peace in Their Time* (1952) and *American Diplomacy in the Great Depression* (1957). (Problem 14)

GEYL, PIETER (1887–1967), historian and educator. After serving as London correspondent for the *Nieuwe Rotterdamsche Courant* during World War I, Geyl became professor of Dutch Studies at London University. He returned to Holland in 1935 to teach at Utrecht University. His works include *Napoleon, For and Against* (1949); *Debates with Historians* (1958); *The Netherlands in the Seventeenth Century* (1961); and *Encounters in History* (1961). (Problem 10)

GIPSON, LAWRENCE HENRY (1880—), historian and educator. The setting of Oxford University and Gipson's personal associations with its faculty members inspired him in his studies of the past. His interest in pre-Revolutionary War history developed at Yale Graduate School where he was a student of Charles M. Andrews. Gipson's *The Triumphant Empire* (1961), volume ten of his *The British Empire Before the American Revolution* (1936–1961), won the 1962 Pulitzer Prize for history. His other writings include *Lewis Evans* (1939) and *The Coming of the Revolution, 1763–1775* (1954). (Problems 3, 5)

GRATTAN, CLINTON HARTLEY (1902—), biographer and critic. During the forty years that he was a free-lance writer of literary, educational, economic, and social affairs, Grattan traveled extensively throughout Australia and the surrounding area. In 1964 he joined the faculty of the University of Texas as a history professor and the curator of his southwest Pacific collection. Grattan's major works include *Why We Fought* (1929); *In Quest of Knowledge* (1955); and *The Southwest Pacific to 1900* (1963). (Problems 11, 15)

HACKER, LOUIS MORTON (1899—), historian. An economics professor at Columbia University, Hacker emphasized the connection between political and economic developments in his writings on United States history. He was graduated from Columbia in 1922. His books include *A Short History of the New Deal* (1934); *The United States: A Graphic History* (1937); and *The Triumph of American Capitalism* (1940). (Problem 2)

JAMESON, JOHN FRANKLIN (1859–1937), historian. In his student days at Amherst, Jameson realized the importance of having historical materials easily accessible. When he became managing editor of the *American Historical Review,* he devoted much time to making such materials available to students of history. In 1905 Jameson was appointed director of the bureau of historical research at the Carnegie Institution of Washington, D.C. and, later, head of the manuscript division of the Library of Congress. His books include *Willem Usselinx* (1887); *History of Historical Writing in America* (1891); and *The American Revolution Considered as a Social Movement* (1926). (Problem 5)

KENNAN, GEORGE FROST (1904—), American diplomat. Kennan, who had had wide experience in the Foreign Service, was assigned to the American Embassy when it reopened in Moscow in 1933. From 1935 to 1944 Kennan's posts included Prague, Berlin, Lisbon, and Moscow. As postwar director of the policy planning staff of the Department of State, Kennan helped formulate the policy of containment in regard to the U.S.S.R. In 1961 he was appointed ambassador to Yugoslavia. His works include *Russia Leaves the War* (1956), which won the 1957 Pulitzer Prize for history; *Russia, the Atom and the West* (1958); and *Russia and the West Under Lenin and Stalin* (1961). (Problems 13, 15)

LIPPMANN, WALTER (1899—), journalist. During his school days, Lippmann wrote articles which strongly advocated socialism. Later, he became disillusioned about the possibility of social planning. In 1914 he helped found the *New Republic* and wrote for that journal until he joined the staff of the New York *World* in 1921. His column "Today and Tomorrow," which began in the New York *Herald Tribune* in 1931, received the 1957 Pulitzer Prize Special Citation and the 1962 Pulitzer Prize for international reporting. His books include *The Good Society* (1937); *U.S. War Aims* (1944); and *The Communist World and Ours* (1959). (Problems 13, 15)

MAY, ERNEST RICHARD (1928—), historian. Because of his study of diplomatic history in college, May was assigned to the historical section of the Joint Chiefs of Staff during the Korean War. He joined the faculty of Harvard in 1954 and was awarded a professorship in 1963. His works include *The World War and American Isolation, 1914–1917* (1959) and *Imperial Democracy: The Emergence of America as a Great Power* (1961). (Problem 15)

MILLER, JOHN CHESTER (1907—), historian. After receiving his Ph.D. from Harvard in 1939, Miller taught at Bryn Mawr College. In 1950 he was appointed Robinson professor of United States history at Stanford University. His works include *Alexander Hamilton: Portrait in Paradox* (1959); *Origins of the American Revolution* (1959); and *The Federalist Era, 1789–1801* (1960). (Problem 4)

MORGAN, EDMUND SEARS (1916—), historian. Morgan was formally educated at Harvard University and received his Ph.D. in 1942. Before he joined the history department at Yale University in 1955, he taught at the University of Chicago and at Brown University. His works include *The Birth of the Republic, 1763–1789* (1956); *The Puritan Dilemma* (1958); and *The Gentle Puritan* (1962). (Problem 5)

NEVINS, ALLAN (1890—), historian and biographer, began his literary career as an editor for the New York *Evening Post* in 1913. His interest in historical personages led him to write of social and economic events in relation to historical personalities. For example, Nevins discussed the rise of big business in America through the biographies of Henry Ford and John D. Rockefeller. Nevins' biographical works include *Grover Cleveland: A Study in Courage* (1932); *Hamilton Fish* (1936); and *The Emergence of Lincoln* (1950). (Problems 7, 9, 10)

NYE, GERALD PRENTICE (1892—), publisher and politician. Nye began his political career in 1925 after fourteen years as a newspaper editor and publisher. He served as a (Progressive) Republican Senator from North Dakota from 1925–1945, becoming known for his leadership of the Senate committee investigating the Teapot Dome Scandal in 1927 and of the Senate Munitions Investigating Committee (Nye Committee) in 1934–1936. A co-sponsor of the Neutrality Act of 1936, Nye continued to support his policy of extreme isolationism even after the United States entered World War II. He was defeated for re-election in 1944. (Problems 11, 15)

OSTERWEIS, ROLLIN (1907—), historian and educator. An early interest in history, international relations, and debating ultimately led Rollin Osterweis into an academic career. A few years after graduation from Yale University, he entered his family's long-established business of cigar manufacturing. During World War II he was assigned to the Navy V-12 program as instructor in history. In 1944 he became Director of Debating and Public Speaking at Yale. His works include *Romanticism and Nationalism in the Old South* (1949) and *Three Centuries of New Haven, 1638–1938* (1953). (Problem 7)

PAINE, THOMAS (1737–1809), edited the *Pennsylvania Magazine* after he emigrated to America from England in 1774. An able propagandist, Paine's political writings not only championed the cause of American independence but also inspired patriotism in the sometimes hesitant Revolutionary troops. His pamphlet *Common Sense* (1776) strongly influenced Americans toward independence. From 1787 to 1802 Paine attempted to foster republican forms of government in England and France, and as a result, was tried for treason and outlawed in England. He was later imprisoned in

France. Claiming Paine as a United States citizen, James Monroe, United States Minister to France, negotiated his release. Among Paine's other writings are *The Rights of Man* (1791, 1792) and *The Age of Reason* (1794, 1796). (Problem 4)

POTTER, DAVID MORRIS (1910—), historian, received his Ph.D. from Yale in 1940. From 1942 to 1961, Potter was a member of the history department at Yale, receiving the appointment of Coe professor of history in 1950. He became the Coe professor at Stanford University in 1961. Potter has written *Lincoln and His Party in the Secession Crisis* (1942) and *People of Plenty* (1954). (Problem 10)

RANDALL, JAMES GARFIELD (1881-1953), historian. Interest in the administrative problems of the Civil War led Randall to an extensive study of Abraham Lincoln as an executive. Among Randall's volumes on Lincoln, *Midstream* (1952) won the Loubat First Prize at Columbia University in 1953. His other Lincoln volumes include *Lincoln, the President* (1945); *Lincoln and the South* (1946); and *Lincoln the Liberal Statesman* (1947). (Problems 8, 9, 10)

SCHLESINGER, ARTHUR MEIER (1888—), historian. As editor of his college newspaper, Schlesinger had envisioned a career in journalism, but his interest in historical research led him to record the past as well as the present. In his long and productive career he taught at Ohio State University, the University of Iowa, and Harvard. In his writings Schlesinger emphasized political events, social evolution, and economic factors. His works include *Learning How To Behave* (1946); *Paths to the Present* (1949); *The American As Reformer* (1950); and *Prelude to Independence* (1958). (Problems 2, 5)

SCHLESINGER, ARTHUR MEIER, JR. (1917—), historian, developed an interest in combating communism while serving with the Office of Strategic Services during World War II. While teaching at Harvard University after the war, he participated in the founding of Americans for Democratic Action. In 1961 he was appointed Special Assistant to the President of the United States. His writings include *The Age of Jackson* (1945), which won the 1946 Pulitzer Prize for history; *The Vital Center* (1949); and *The Age of Roosevelt* (1957-1962). (Problems 9, 10.)

SEYMOUR, CHARLES (1885-1963), historian and educator. Seymour's discussion of the causes of World War I in *The Diplomatic Background of the War* (1916) so impressed President Woodrow Wilson that he appointed Seymour to the American Commission to Negotiate Peace. Later, Wilson selected him as a delegate to the Paris Peace Conference. Seymour commenced teaching at Yale in 1911; in 1918 he became a professor, and in 1937 he was appointed president of the university. His writings include *American Diplomacy During the World War* (1934) and *American Neutrality, 1914-1917* (1935). (Problems 12, 15)

SMITH, PAGE (1917—), historian. A search for activities to pass the time while convalescing from wounds incurred during World War II led Page Smith to a study of historical trends. After his recovery, he persuaded the Harvard administration to allow him to do his graduate work in history, although he had never had a history course. In 1962 Smith was appointed professor of history at the University of California at Los Angeles. Smith is the author of *John Adams* (1962) and *The Historian and History* (1964). (Problem 5)